Nancy Cornwell's
Polar Magic

Published by

700 E. State St.
Iola, WI 54990-0001
Telephone 715-445-2214
www.krause.com

Please call or write for our free catalog of publications. Our toll-free number to place an order or obtain a free catalog is 800-258-0929 or please use our regular business telephone, 715-445-2214.

Library of Congress Catalog Number: 2001090426

ISBN: 0-87349-256-0

Printed in the United States of America

The following company or product names appear in this book:

Brother Pacesetter™ (Brother International), Cactus Punch, Inc., Candlelight (YLI Corp.), Chacopel Pencils (Clover Needlecraft, Inc.), Citifleece™ and Kinderfleece™ (Dyersburg Corp.), Elna EnVision Clothsetter III (Elna USA), Faux Chenille™ (Nanette Holmberg), Golden Threads™ Quilting Paper, Golden Threads™ Strippy Quilt Pack®, Lycra™ (DuPont Co.), Mesh Transfer Canvas (Clover Needlecraft, Inc.), Mini Iron™ (Clover Needlecraft, Inc.), Mylar, Nordic™ Fleece (David Textiles, Inc.), Omnistrips™ (Omnigrid®, Inc.), Paw Prints Pattern Co.® (Purrfection Artistic Wearables®), Pelle's See Thru Stamps™ (Purrfection Artistic Wearables®), Pfaff (Pfaff American Sales Corp.), Polarfleece® and Polartec® (Malden Mills), Purrfection Artistic Wearables®, Quick Bias Design & Appliqué Sheet™ (Clover Needlecraft, Inc.), Quilt Sew Easy (Heavenly Notions), Solar™ Fleece (Siltex Mills), Sulky® KK2000™ Temporary Adhesive Spray (Gunold + Stykma), Sulky® Soft 'n Sheer™ (Gunold + Stykma), Sulky® Solvy™ (Gunold + Stykma), Sulky® Super Solvy™ (Gunold + Stykma), Sulky® Totally Stable™ (Gunold + Stykma), Sulky® Ultra Solvy™ (Gunold + Stykma), Teflon, UltraSuede® (Toray UltraSuede {America}, Inc.), Viking Sewing Machines, Inc., Wash-Away Wonder Tape (W.H. Collins, Inc.), Yukon Fleece™ (Huntingdon Mills).

DEDICATION

To my husband, Jeff.

I thank you for always being there for me.

You are constantly supportive and patient,
especially when I bite off more than I can chew.

You willingly manage the rest of "our world"
while I create, experiment, design, write, and
edit.

You are truly the "wind beneath my wings"

   … and my best friend.

ACKNOWLEDGMENTS

Polar Magic is written in my words, but it is the result of the help, support, and encouragement of so many people. From the bottom of my heart, I extend my thanks…

To you, my readers and friends, for your flattering response to my first two books and the ideas I presented. Your excitement and support made those books a tremendous success. And as *Polar Magic* shows, I truly enjoy and accept your challenge to continually discover new ways to play with fleece.

To David Textiles, Inc., especially David Cohen and Bert Levy, who offered me the chance to stretch my wings and grow in many directions in the sewing industry. Besides working in Sales and Marketing with all kinds of textiles, I have the opportunity to design Nordic fleece prints, work with manufacturers, travel the country, present seminars, write books and magazine features, and film television shows. It's been a mutually satisfying and rewarding association for all of us, and I appreciate the opportunity you have given me.

To Beth Ann Bruske, Creative Director of David Textiles, Inc. for helping me turn my fleece ideas into reality, and especially for making my designs look as good on cloth as they did in my head. (There is a lot that happens between the concept stage and the actual printed fleece design.)

To the Krause Publications folks, who, bless their hearts, early in 1997 told me, "You need to write a book on fleece." Thankfully, they hounded me until I said yes, and the rest is a fun and fleece-filled history. And a special thanks goes to Barbara Case, my editor, who makes me look good "in print" and to photographer Ross Hubbard, who makes my fleece looks good "on paper."

To Viking Sewing Machines, Inc. for providing state of the art sewing machines that offer so many opportunities to experiment and play… and succeed. And for their continued support in all my ventures.

To my "rescuers:" Bruce Lund, Shari Hopple, and Gaylen Matlock of Viking Sewing Center in Lynnwood, Wash. They enthusiastically jump in with both feet to answer my "Viking" questions, help problem solve, keep my machine purring, and give me honest opinions and input whenever I ask. Whenever I cry "help," they drop whatever they are doing and rescue me. Thanks for all your help.

To Sulky of America for listening to the home sewer and continually offering innovative new products and techniques. Sulky truly helps us to "play" with our sewing machines and enjoy this wonderful hobby.

To Lindee and Bill Goodall of Cactus Punch, Inc. for providing a phenomenal choice of fantastic embroidery designs to the home sewer. I thank you for encouraging me to expand my ideas and giving me the opportunity to design the Signature Series #45 embroidery motifs especially for fleece.

To Clover Needlecraft, Inc. and Prym-Dritz Corp. for providing creative sewers with so many notions that make our lives so much easier.

To Dana Bontrager, of Purrfection Artistic Wearables, for agreeing to write a guest chapter for this book. Her expertise on heat and ink stamping translate beautifully to fleece.

To Jeanine Twigg, industry sport snap expert, national speaker, and author of *Embroidery Machine Essentials,* for being a great friend. Besides giving the industry the first comprehensive and authoritative book on machine embroidery, she's been a great "wall" to bounce ideas and problems off of.

And to Malden Mills Industries, Inc. for starting the whole fleece craze that has kept our country warm (and fashionable) for more than 30 years. Your products set the standard for quality and performance.

Last, but not least, I have to acknowledge Bob and Molly, our two precious RagaMuffin cats, who intricately incorporated themselves into every aspect of this book. They curled on the computer table, on top of my notes, purring contentedly while I wrote. They kept me warm by wrapping themselves around my feet, whether at the computer desk, editing table, or sewing machine. They snuggled deeply into partially sewn fleece projects. They sprawled across the cutting table and constantly rearranged every pattern piece in sight. They attacked every tidbit of fleece that happened to peek over the edge of my sewing table and helpfully removed fleece scraps from the waste basket in case those tidbits were in there by mistake. They thoroughly enjoyed this whole project and continually made me smile.

OREWORD

The only thing that surpasses Nancy Cornwell's creativity with fleece is her ability to share her great ideas, techniques, and projects for sewing fleece with others. As my guest on "America Sews with Sue Hausmann," Nancy taught me the "tip of the iceberg" and I have so appreciated her innovative books to teach me "sew" much more!

Nancy's first two books, *Adventures with Polarfleece®* and *More Polarfleece® Adventures* give step-by-step instructions for a number of ways to sew one-of-a-kind fleece garments and gifts with a personal touch. The best part is that the projects are quick and easy to sew, thanks to Nancy's clear instructions.

As the popularity of sewing and wearing fleece continues to grow, Nancy has continued to experiment with new notions, fleece types, techniques, and ways to personalize your fleece garments. This third book, *Polar Magic*, reviews and renews fleece basics, teaches how to use "gotta-have" notions, and shows easy ways to transfer designs on this specialty fabric. You'll also learn to sew with the beautiful fleece border prints, create fleece ribbing, trapunto quilt on fleece and much, much more.

"Sew" read through the ideas, techniques, projects, and suggestions. Enjoy as Nancy's enthusiasm for sewing with fleece and sharing her innovative techniques literally jump off the page to inspire you.

Then take a favorite piece of fleece yardage, whether it is from the fabric store or your fabric collection, and put Nancy's tips and ideas into action to create something special for yourself and/or someone you love! Nancy makes sewing fleece a joy!

Happy Sewing!

Sue Hausmann
Senior Vice President Education,
Viking Sewing Machines, Inc.
Host of "America Sews with Sue
Hausmann," PBS television series

TABLE OF CONTENTS

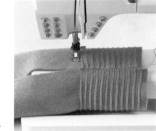

INTRODUCTION

Why another book on playing with fleece?

Because new ideas keep cropping up.

Because companies continually offer new and innovative products that allow us to create different effects.

Because it's fun to explore all the possibilities our sewing machines offer us.

And most of all... Because sewing is about creativity.

The beauty of the sewing world is that there are so many different areas for expressing creativity – quilting, children's sewing, home dec, fleece sewing, embroidery, tailoring, heirloom sewing, textile art, etc. Many of the products, techniques, and methods promoted in one sewing field can easily cross over and be used in other sewing areas. Don't overlook using virtually any technique on fleece. Many techniques take on a wonderful new personality when applied to fleece.

Pintucking using narrow double needles on batiste or linen is called "heirloom" sewing. Pintucking with wider double needles on fleece is called "polar ribbing!"

Trapunto quilting on layers of cotton and batting provides a decorative and functional way to anchor multiple layers together. Adapt that same technique to a single layer of fleece and the result is a new way to embellish with subtle texture.

Much of *Polar Magic* features untraditional applications of traditional sewing techniques.

The techniques I've presented in this book, as well as in *Adventures With Polarfleece®* and *More Polarfleece® Adventures*, are approaches that made sense to me and worked for me. In no way do I suggest that there is only one right way to do things. If you have an idea, or a different approach to a technique, try it. It may well turn out to be a better way of doing it! If it is logical and makes sense, by all means try it! (Some rules are meant to be broken.)

Following the footsteps of the first two books of the series, the techniques presented in *Polar Magic* use fleece as the base fabric. However, most of these ideas work beautifully on any lofted fabric.

I'm no different than creative sewers everywhere. I like to add extra flavor to the garments I sew – some special touches that act as my "signature." It may be a little embellishment, the way a corner is treated, an added seamline for design detail, rounding a corner, or squaring a curve. Some little change that "makes it mine."

Enhancing fleece with texture and embellishment is a wonderful way to inject your personality and style into your garments.

As you make your way through all three of my "playing with fleece" books, keep in mind the different kinds of sewing you already do and apply some of your favorite techniques to fleece. Most of the techniques featured in these books don't reinvent the wheel, they just take the wheel down a different road. That's why this is called.... An Adventure.

So look beyond the obvious. Experiment. Play. Most of all, have fun!

Create your own adventure....

Love,
Marcy

Chapter 1 ❄ REFRESHER COURSE

Don't skip this chapter thinking "been there, done that." This is a condensed overview of important information crucial to successful fleece sewing.

My first book, *Adventures With Polarfleece®*, thoroughly covered all the important principles and sewing techniques for sewing with fleece. I presented in-depth sewing techniques, no-fail zipper applications, buttonhole instruction,

appropriate pattern choices, ready-to-wear edge finishes, seam options, UltraSuede accents, and designer details – everything necessary for successful sewing on fleece and pile fabrics. I am proud this book won Primedia's Best Sewing Book of 1998 Award.

At the end of my first book I began playing with fleece, sculpturing and pintucking, creating textures and designs, adding personality to fleece garments. After a taste of playing, everyone wanted more. So my second book, *More Polarfleece® Adventures*, picked up where the first book left off. I expanded on the concept of sculpturing, branching into double needle sculpturing and free-motion designs. Pintucking for dimension, and "to-die-for" polar ribbing. Cutwork, embroidery, and appliqué. We played and had fun, and we're still having fun!

Polar Magic takes up where the second book left off, offering more fun ideas for putting your personality in fleece garments using texture and embellishment, using untraditional applications of traditional sewing techniques. When I started writing this book, I was ready to just jump in with both feet and take up where I left off at the end of the last book. But... (It seems like there is always a "but.")

New notions have come into the marketplace that make some techniques so much easier. That meant I had additions to my recommended "gotta-have-it" notions list. And, as I traveled across the country speaking and teaching, I kept hearing the same questions being asked over and over again. When I pointed out that the information is in the books, everyone replied, "Can't you just give us a down-and-dirty quick synopsis of the important things to keep in mind at all times?" So...

Golden Rules for Successful Fleece Sewing

1. Loosen up
2. Lighten up
3. Tape it up
4. If the conditions change, the rules change

Short. Sweet. To the point. Easy to remember. These four points are, to me, the most important things to remember for a good-looking fleece garment. If the base garment doesn't look good (if the seams wave, the zippers buckle, the buttonholes gap open, or the hems look bumpy), it doesn't matter what wonderful techniques you do to embellish the garment. Food for thought.

Loosen Up

I should really say "lengthen up," but in this day and age the term "loosen up" seems easier to remember. I am by no means encouraging sewers to be "loose women," rather I am telling you to lengthen the stitch length on both your conventional sewing machine and serger. I cannot stress enough the importance of this simple stitch length adjustment. Increasing the stitch length probably solves 90% of all fleece sewing problems.

If you consider the logic behind longer stitches, you will never again forget to loosen up. Remember how to make ruffled rib – the feminine frilly, lettuce-edged finish on ribbed collars and cuffs shown in the photo? To get the rippled effect, you hold the folded edge of the ribbing between both hands, pull the ribbing taut, and stitch completely over the edge using a wide zigzag satin stitch. In reality, what

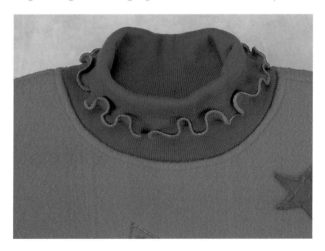

you are doing is sewing incorrectly for a purpose. You stretch the ribbing and cover the edge with stitches. When you let go of the stretched ribbing, it cannot bounce back to its original dimension because there is too much thread piled in. The result is a distorted wavy edge. On ribbing, it looks ruffled and pretty. On garments, it becomes wavy seams and buckled zippers and it looks tacky.

The new battle cry is "Remember ruffled rib." Ribbing is a stretch fabric. So is fleece. The same thing happens if you use a too-short stitch length when sewing hems, seams, zippers, pockets, or buttonholes. If you force in too many stitches, the fleece stretches and waves. Pretty on ribbing... Not pretty in the garment!

nancy's hint

Because this is a fleece book, I address stitch length as it relates to fleece. However, keep this battle cry in mind for all knit sewing. The logic is the same. The results are the same whether you are sewing on interlock, sweatshirt, jersey, knit terry, or velour. If you are working on a stretch knit, lengthen your stitch length.

This means you don't just turn on your machine and sew. Most newer sewing machines have a default stitch length setting of 2.25mm to 2.5mm. This is approximately 12 to 14 stitches per inch. The machine "assumes" you are sewing with a traditional woven fabric, and the stitch length is prescribed accordingly. This shorter stitch length is appropriate for woven fabrics. It is not appropriate for knit fabrics. (Remember ruffled rib.)

When sewing with fleece, adjust your stitch length to at least 3.0 mm, or approximately nine stitches per inch. Personally speaking, I usually stitch at 3.5mm (approximately seven stitches per inch). When facing bulky multiple layers or sewing on the crossgrain "with the stretch," I increase the length to 4.0mm.

nancy's note

This longer stitch length is appropriate for casual fleece garments with no high-stress seams. If sewing a tight-fitting Lycra blend fleece garment, with high stress seams, revert to "Lycra rules" rather than "fleece rules." Shorten the stitch length to 12 to 14 stitches per inch. In the relaxed state the seams may ripple, but when stretched on the body they will be smooth and strong.

Recap

If your seam waves...
If your zipper buckles...
If your buttonhole "frog mouths"...
If your pockets bubble...

Loosen Up! Remember ruffled rib for all your fleece and knit sewing. Nine times out of ten, that's all that's needed. This rule applies to your serger as well. Simple!
Remember ruffled rib!

Lighten Up

Fleece is bulkier than most fabrics in your sewing stash. If you find your fleece balking at feeding through the machine, the first rule is "Loosen Up" (lengthen your stitch length). This makes the feed teeth move in larger increments and helps feed the fabric through.

If a longer stitch length does not help the fleece feed through, then "Lighten Up." Lessen the pressure on the presser foot. You might have been considering tightening the pressure to force the fleece through. No. Lessen the pressure to allow the fleece to feed through. The lighter pressure also reduces any tendency of fleece layers to shift alignment.

Tape It Up

Always have Wash-Away Wonder Tape on hand. (Personally, I always have two on hand to be safe.) This double-sided, wash-away, stitch-through tape is a godsend for so many applications. Don't waste time pinning when you can tape with better success.

Tape zippers in place for perfect, flat zippers every time. (Read the No-Hassle Zippers chapter in *Adventures With Polar-fleece®* for detailed instructions on a variety of zipper applications and treatments.)

Tape pockets or decorative trim in place for perfect alignment. Use this tape to match plaids, hold appliqués, and hold lapped seams.

If the Conditions Change, the Rules Change

This rule seems all too obvious when you say it, yet in the everyday sequence of sewing, we rarely think about it. Its most important application is probably in connection with needle choices. When you read the information regarding needles, consider the guidelines given as a starting point, subject to change as conditions dictate.

Choose the needle *size* according to the weight of the fabric sewn. Choose the needle *type* according to the fabric type, thread choice, and type of sewing you are doing. For example, if you are sewing on a mid-weight fleece using the recommended 90/14 needle, and all of a sudden you have an area where you are stitching through three or four layers of fleece, you should change to a larger 100/16 needle size. The medium size needle handled the medium weight fleece under normal conditions, but the added weight and bulk of multiple layers may cause the needle to bend and skip stitches or to break.

As for needle type, choose a universal or ball-point needle because you are sewing on fleece,

which is a knit fabric. If applying UltraSuede trim onto fleece, alter your needle choice to fit the demands of UltraSuede. UltraSuede is fussier than fleece and sews nicer with a stretch needle. If topstitching with metallic thread on UltraSuede on fleece, choose a needle type to accommodate metallic thread (generally a 90/14 metallic, embroidery, or topstitch needle). Because metallic thread is fussier than UltraSuede, which is fussier than fleece, you should choose the needle type according to the metallic thread demands.

In other words, choose the needle type according to the fussiest element of your sewing.

Fabric Basics

Polyester fleece comes in a wide range of colors, prints, textures, qualities, and prices. Fleece can be produced domestically or imported from the Orient. Quality ranges from trademarked brands to generic brands.

The most recognized trademarked names (also the highest quality) are Polarfleece and Polartec from Malden Mills (USA), Nordic Fleece from David Textiles, Inc. (imported), Citifleece and Kinderfleece from Dyersburg Corp. (USA), Solar Fleece from Siltex Mills (Canada), and Yukon Fleece from Huntingdon Mills (Canada).

Fabric & Garment Care

Pre-treatment: No need to pre-treat fleece since it does not shrink or shed excess color. You can buy it and sew it immediately!

Laundering: Avoid unnecessary abrasion by washing the garment inside out, with similar garments. Use a powdered detergent, lukewarm water, and the gentle cycle. Do not use bleach or any type of softener agent (liquid or dryer sheets). Toss in the dryer on low heat for a short time.

Pressing: Not recommended. If, during the construction stage, pressing seems necessary, hold the iron above the fabric and steam. Then gently finger press to encourage the fleece to lay in the desired position. Never place an iron in direct contact with fleece. Direct contact may leave a permanent imprint on the fleece.

Which Is the Right Side?

To find the right side of fleece, stretch along the cut edge, on the crossgrain (the direction of most stretch). With few exceptions, fleece curls to the *wrong* side.

Remember: Fleece pulled along the cut edge on the crossgrain (most stretch) curls to the wrong side. Remember this rule. You'll use it a lot.

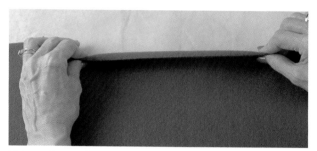

This "curl test" shows the wrong side facing up and the right side against the table.

If, after using this test, you really want what tests to be the wrong side, pre-treat the fleece to see how it looks after laundering. If you still prefer the wrong side, by all means go ahead and use it.

nancy's disclaimer

There will be times throughout the book when I instruct you to iron a stabilizer to the wrong side of the fleece so you can do specific techniques. In these cases, use a dry iron and a light touch. The iron should never come in direct contact with the fleece, but rather touch only the stabilizer.

nancy's note

After you've determined which is the right side of the fleece, be religious and meticulous about marking the right side on every cut-out garment piece. (Chacopel pencils are a good choice for marking fleece.) These "right side marks" are a great help during construction.

nancy's important note

There are many times throughout this book when you are handling a "piece" of fleece (a square, a patch, an appliqué) and you need to determine the right side of the fabric. Since it is only a piece, you have no selvage as a reference for determining the crossgrain of fabric.

To determine the right and wrong side of a piece of fleece, gently pull on the cut edges for both directions of the piece. Fleece has decidedly more stretch on the crossgrain. After determining the direction of most stretch, tug along the cut edge with the most stretch and the fleece will curl to the wrong side.

Sewing Basics for Sewing Machine & Serger

Make sure your machines are cleaned, oiled, and in good working order. Sewing with fleece accumulates a lot of lint. Clean frequently.

Thread

Choose good quality, long staple polyester thread to match your fleece color or a shade darker. This is not the time to be tempted with bargain threads that will easily fray and break.

Needles

Always begin a project with a fresh, new needle.

Because fleece is a knitted fabric, choose a universal, stretch, or ballpoint needle. These needles have rounded points that deflect rather than pierce the yarn.

Choose needle size according to the weight of the fleece you are using. Use the smallest size possible that is strong enough to do the job.

Recommended Sizes:
Lightweight fleece: 70/10 or 75/11
Mid-weight fleece: 80/12 or 90/14
Heavyweight fleece: 100/16

Choose the needle type according to the fabric type, thread choice, and type of sewing you are doing. Choose the needle type according to the fussiest element of your sewing.

For in-depth fleece fabric information and fleece construction techniques, please read *Adventures With Polarfleece®*.

General Guidelines:
Regular construction sewing: Universal, ballpoint, or stretch needle
Rayon thread: Embroidery needle
Metallic thread: Metallic, topstitch, or embroidery needle, size 90/14 or larger

nancy's hint

If you experience skipped stitches or a broken needle, go up one needle size.

nancy's reminder

If the conditions change, the rules change. It never fails to amaze me how many machine problems are corrected by a simple needle change.

Chapter 2
GOTTA-HAVE NOTIONS
(TO MAKE YOUR LIFE EASIER)

Woodworkers need different saws and tools to accomplish various tasks and achieve a variety of effects. Artists need different brushes and paints to portray their subjects. Creative sewers need an assortment of notions to make sewing techniques easier and finished garments look more professional.

This chapter offers a wide range of sewing notions and tools to help make your sewing experience more enjoyable. Some are oldies-but-goodies mentioned in my earlier books, some are newcomers to the market.

I mention the following products throughout the book because I have used them and have been pleased with their performance. I choose notions that are readily available at your local fabric store, quilt shop, or favorite sewing machine dealer. There may be similar products available that will work just as well.

Adventures With Polarfleece® by Nancy Cornwell

This is an obviously biased opinion, but I am proud of this book, as it has become acknowledged as the sewing industry's "polar encyclopedia." This is the resource handbook to turn to for in-depth fleece information, sewing machine and serger techniques, what to look for in patterns, seam options, ready-to-wear edge finishes, no-hassle zipper applications ranging from practical everyday zippers to designer applications, buttonholes (standard, fashion, and troubleshooting), UltraSuede accents, plus an introduction to sculpturing and texturing fleece. Included are projects to sew.

More Polarfleece® Adventures by Nancy Cornwell

(Another obviously biased opinion.) While I am proud of the first book, I had a ball writing the second book. It is playing – pure and simple. Putting flavor and style into fleece with texturizing, pintucking, sculpturing, and embellishing. Injecting your personality into your sewing. Sculpturing

with double needles, sculpturing with decorative stitches, echo stitching, free-motion sculpturing, pintucking cascades and plaids, framing, polar ribbing (the hit of the book), classy cutwork, embroidery challenges and solutions, appliqué techniques, more buttonholes and edge finishes. The book concludes with Scrap Happy, a chapter devoted to making good use of leftover fleece scraps.

Wash-A-Way Wondertape, Double-Sided Basting Tape from Collins

I continually refer to this product because it can be used for so many applications. I choose this product because the 1/4" width has terrific holding power, you can sew through it without gumming up the needle, and because it doesn't need to be removed – it launders away! Look for the words "wash away" to be sure you have the correct product.

It's perfect for holding garment pieces in place where pins would be awkward. Because it prevents shifting of layers, it is the only way to "baste" zippers and pockets in place. It is also very convenient to spot hold appliqués and decorative trims.

Long Glass Head or Flower Head Pins

Pins can easily get buried or lost in the loft of fleece. For best visibility (thus avoiding unwanted contact with serger blades), choose longer pins. When pinning, place pins at a 90° angle to the seamline or cut edges.

Chacopel Pencils from Clover

Chacopel pencils are my favorite fabric-marking pencils because they mark easily on fleece and stay marked until I rub it away. I find other marking tools are either too difficult to see or they rub off too easily when handling the fabric.

Caution: Sharpen these pencils to a *medium* point. Do not over-sharpen, as a fine point breaks too easily.

Mesh Transfer Canvas from Clover

This handy notion makes transferring designs and motifs onto fleece a very simple process. In my first two books, depending on the size of the motif and how I was going to stitch it, I used Totally Stable or Solvy for transferring design lines to sew on fleece. Mesh transfer canvas provides an alternative way to transfer most motifs

Mesh transfer canvas is a 12" x 16" piece of fine gauge plastic mesh. It has the benefit of being reusable over and over again. Simply lay the mesh canvas over the desired motif and trace. Use a Chacopel or regular pencil if you want to reuse the canvas. Use a permanent pen if you want it to serve as a permanent template.

Then lay the traced mesh canvas on your fleece and redraw the design using Chacopel pencils. The pencil easily marks through the little mesh holes onto the fleece! Quick and easy.

Need to reverse the design? Simply flip the traced mesh canvas over. Voilá! No need to use a light box or sunny window to mirror image and reverse motifs.

Quilting Paper from Golden Threads

You'll find many uses for this lightweight but strong seven-pound vellum. It offers a terrific no-marking method of transferring designs for embellishment like sculpturing, texturizing, and trapunto. Originally designed for making quilting templates (single motifs and continuous designs), it is perfect for transferring designs onto fleece.

Golden Threads Quilting Paper is much lighter weight than other similar products. Because it is so sheer, it is easy to see through to trace designs and it tears away completely clean without distorting stitches or leaving tons of paper eyelashes to pick out. It is a light golden color so it is easy to see on all fabric colors.

It comes in 20-yard rolls, in widths of 12", 18", and 24", making it perfect to use for continuous designs.

It's ideal for sculpturing, couching, trapunto, appliqué, machine embroidery, and duplicating designs.

Totally Stable from Sulky

Totally Stable is a temporary iron-on tear-away stabilizer. I use it to stabilize fleece for sculpturing, cutwork, and other embellishment techniques that might stretch or distort the fabric. It is also great for transferring designs.

Use a dry iron when adhering Totally Stable to the wrong side of the fleece. Some stabilizer will remain in the stitches, so use it only when the underside of the work will not be visible.

Totally Stable is available in black or white.

nancy's hints

#1. When adhering Totally Stable, remember that it is only a temporary bonding. Set the iron temperature appropriate for the fabric used. Use only enough heat and pressure to adhere the stabilizer. If the iron is too hot or if you over-press, the hold will be too strong. The stabilizer will then be difficult to remove and you risk "defleecing" the fabric. It's better to under-press and go back to touch up as necessary.

#2. When removing tear-away stabilizer, place one hand along the stitches and with the other hand, tear at a 45° angle to the stitching line. Imagine the age-old instruction, "tear along the dotted line." This will prevent possible distortion of the stitches.

#3. Another easy removal tip is to use a pointed object (serger tweezers, seam ripper point, small screwdriver) and score the Totally Stable alongside the stitches. This scoring releases the hold and allows easy removal.

Soft 'n Sheer from Sulky

This lovely, soft, cut-away permanent stabilizer is an excellent backing for many techniques where you need the stabilizer to remain permanently in the technique. Because it is soft, it is comfortable against the skin. Because it is lightweight, it doesn't interfere with the hand of the fleece and does not add bulk. It can be layered for those times when perhaps a bit more stabilization is required.

Soft 'n Sheer is available in black or white.

Solvy from Sulky

Solvy is a water-soluble stabilizer perfect for a wide array of techniques. I use Solvy to create good-looking buttonholes, to transfer designs, as a stabilizer for cutwork, and as a topping for embroidery. It rinses away with warm water. It is also available as Super Solvy (two times heavier than Solvy) and Ultra Solvy (four times heavier).

KK2000 Temporary Adhesive Spray from Sulky

This innovative product is the solution to many "holding" predicaments. It is used extensively throughout my books to make a wide variety of applications and techniques much easier. The beauty of this spray adhesive is that it absorbs into the fibers in two or three days and completely disappears in three to ten days. (The timing depends on the amount sprayed, fabric type, heat, humidity, and air circulation.) The simple explanation: The molecular structure breaks down, not allowing the chemicals, glue, and propellant to harden. There will be absolutely no residue remaining on the fabric.

This heavier-than-air propellant is not petroleum based, so it is not flammable. Because the spray is heavy, you can hold the can as close as 6" to 10" from your fabric. It goes exactly where you want it without wasteful overspray.

nancy's hints

#1. When tracing a design onto Solvy, use a water erase marker, air erase marker, or fine-line permanent pen. If using a pen, make sure it is permanent ink. (My heart was in my stomach the first time I traced with permanent ink. I was nervous because I didn't want permanent ink on my fabric! However, the permanent ink adheres only to the Solvy. When rinsed away, it rinses away, too!)

#2. If I am going to be stitching over Solvy traced with permanent ink, I choose an ink color that matches or blends with the thread color. That way, if it takes more than one rinsing to entirely remove the Solvy, any trace ink blends in with the stitching.

#3. Pay careful attention to the KK2000 Caution #3 on page 19 regarding using KK2000 with Solvy.

nancy's comment

The two most important reasons I use choose KK2000 are the terrific holding power using minimal spray and the control you have over the spray, without overspray.

NOTE: KK2000 is not water-soluble. It does not wash out or rinse away. It does not want any contact with water. It is formulated to dissolve on its own. Do not interfere with the process. Pay close attention to Caution #3 on page 19.

Important KK2000 Caution #1: Spray KK2000 on the surface that will be removed rather than onto the fleece itself.

For example, lightly spray KK2000 adhesive on the stabilizer and then adhere to the fleece. Or lightly spray KK2000 on the Solvy and then adhere to the fleece. When the stabilizer or the Solvy is removed, most of the adhesive will be removed with it, leaving only a trace amount on the fleece (which disappears over time.) Spray the KK2000 onto trim or an appliqué, and then adhere to the fleece. This keeps the adhesive exactly where you want it with no room for error.

Important KK2000 Caution #2: Spray lightly. KK2000 has terrific holding power and does not need to be heavily applied. Excessive adhesive takes much longer to disappear.

Important KK2000 Caution #3: KK2000 dissolves and goes away on its own. Any interference risks a gummy result that will be difficult to remove. Don't try to wash it out – it's not water-soluble.

In some techniques I spray Solvy with KK2000 adhesive and adhere it to the fleece. Although Solvy rinses away with warm water, if you rinse the Solvy-adhered fleece, you will get a gummy residue (because KK2000 is not water-soluble). It is important to first peel off the adhesive-sprayed Solvy. The little bits remaining in the stitches won't present a problem when later rinsed away. I still allow time for the remaining hint of adhesive to disappear before rinsing.

Important KK2000 Caution #4: Machine manufacturers recommend that when applying any spray adhesive, you work in an area totally removed from your conventional sewing machine, serger, and embroidery machine. This precautionary step ensures that no adhesive comes in contact with the tension discs or any other sensitive machine mechanism. Better safe than sorry!

Embroidery Machine Essentials
by Jeanine Twigg

There are a number of times throughout this book where I play with embroidery machine designs, adapting them to texturize and embellish fleece. I'm not doing embroidery the "real" way, I'm cheating a little. And the rule is: Know the correct technique before you cheat.

Refer to *Embroidery Machine Essentials* by industry embroidery expert Jeanine Twigg for authoritative and comprehensive information on everything you need to know for successful machine embroidery. The book covers the entire embroidery process, from choosing designs, threads, stabilizers, and needles to hooping, design placement, and stitching technique. All the major machine brands are represented. (It even includes a free CD with exclusive designs!)

"Adventures With Fleece" Embroidery Designs from Cactus Punch

Cactus Punch, Inc. is one of the best-known suppliers of embroidery designs in the country. They digitize embroidery motifs for both the home sewing and commercial markets. The designs for home embroidery machines come on a CD, formatted for use in any machine.

Lindee Goodall, the creative force behind Cactus Punch, suggested that I design an embroidery card with designs geared around use on fleece – simpler, more open designs that played up the contrast between the loft of the fleece and the depth of the stitches. So I designed "Signature Series #45 – Adventures With Fleece" that offers 20 embroidery designs with 89 variations! Snowflakes and leaves (that reflect the same print found in the fleece border prints), paw prints, trees, birds, and more. The motifs can be used on any fabric but are especially effective when used on lofted fabrics like fleece, quilted cotton, sweatshirting, velour, etc.

Omnistrips Cutting Mats from Omnigrid

These long skinny mini cutting mats are designed for easy cutting in tiny places. They are perfect for making fleece Faux Chenille. The strips come in a variety of sizes from 1/4" to 5/8".

Quilt Sew Easy Hoops from Heavenly Notions

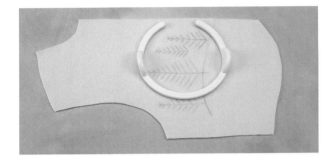

Originally designed as an aid for free-motion quilting, this flexible hoop is perfect for the free-motion sculpturing on page 70. It removes the fear factor from that group of "free-motion impaired" sewers (like me) who panic when the feed teeth are lowered.

Quilt Sew Easy consists of a flexible crescent-shaped hoop (two sizes, 6-1/2" and 8", come in the package) with foam pads on the underside for non-skid fabric handling. It is also a great tool to use when stitch-stenciling multiple layers of Quilting Paper (page 30).

If your general fabric store does not carry Quilt Sew Easy hoops, check a quilt fabric shop or your favorite sewing machine dealer.

Cutting Tools

Treat yourself to high quality cutting tools, and preserve their sharp edges by restricting them to use in your sewing room only. The results are definitely worth it!

Rotary cutters. Rotary cutters are available from several companies. Bulky fleeces are much easier to cut when using the larger size 60mm cutter. The larger blade effortlessly handles the bulk while the corresponding larger handle is comfortable to use. (I now use the larger blade for all my cutting needs.) For specialty edge finishes, choose the medium 45mm rotary cutter with specialty blades (wave, pinking, etc.).

Appliqué Scissors. With the flat disc-shaped underside blade, these scissors offer close accurate trimming of a top layer while protecting the remaining underlayer of fabric from unintentional nicks and cuts.

Embroidery Scissors. These come in a variety of sizes and shapes. They have very sharp points for accurate trimming in close quarters. They can be flat, curved, or bent.

Mini Iron from Clover

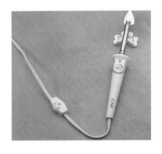

This is one of those obvious "Why didn't I think of that?" inventions you will use in so many ways. It's a great little tool to have alongside your sewing machine (no more running back and forth to the ironing board!) for pressing seams open, whether quilting or tailoring. It eliminates the hassle of getting into corners when turning collars and cuffs. It easily goes places your household iron can't fit. And if you love stained glass appliqué, this is the only way to go!

Aside from all the practical uses listed above, I fell in love with the mini iron because it finally gave me a method for applying heat-activated adhesive trim to fleece. The small tip on the mini iron makes it easy to press trims and appliqués onto fleece without the danger of flattening the fleece nap – something you can't avoid with the large sole plate of a traditional iron.

The Mini Iron has multiple temperature settings, making it versatile for many applications.

Quick Bias from Clover

This delightful trim comes in a large range of colors – cotton solids and sparkly polyester metallics. The ease of embellishing with adhesive-backed quick bias trim is almost too good to be true, but up until now, adhering it to fleece had been a problem. The Mini Iron now offers an easy way to apply Quick Bias to fleece without risking damage to the nap of the fleece.

Quick Bias Design & Appliqué Sheet from Clover

This reusable sheet is a gotta-have to make things even easier with the Mini Iron and the adhesive Quick Bias. Instead of trying to arrange Quick Bias in a design on your garment, this sheet allows you to pre-make the design. Lay the Appliqué Sheet over the motif you want to make from the Quick Bias (it's easy to see through). Use the Mini Iron to press the trim in place. Let cool, then lift off the finished motif and you are ready to "Mini Iron" it onto your fleece project!

Chapter 3

Transferring Designs

OR
"How do I get there from here?"

The beauty of the sewing world is that there are so many different areas for expressing creativity – quilting, children's sewing, home dec, fleece sewing, embroidery, tailoring, textile art, etc. So many of the products, techniques, and methods promoted in one art can easily cross over and be used in other sewing arenas. The transferring techniques listed here are taken from various areas of sewing and applied to fleece creativity.

Don't skip this section because you've read some of this in Adventures With Polarfleece® or More Polarfleece® Adventures. New transferring techniques, products, and approaches have been added. Rather than sprinkling them throughout the book, I decided to include them in one chapter for easy reference. While I am recommending these techniques for fleece sewing, do not overlook them for all your creative sewing.

Listed in this chapter are a variety of methods for transferring designs and motifs onto fleece so you can stitch, sculpture, pintuck, couch yarns, free-motion embroider, trapunto, or otherwise "dress up" your fabric. There is no one right way. Choose whatever method you prefer. Your choice of method will change according to the size of the motif, how you are going to embellish it, and what notions you happen to have in your stash at the time. If you run out of one stabilizer or transfer material, don't worry, there is always another method that will work.

nancy's note

Listed on the following pages are numerous ways of transferring motifs onto fleece as a guideline for embellishment. Depending on the embellishment that will be done, it may be necessary to take additional preparatory steps. For example, if you are going to sculpture stitch a motif, it's necessary to first stabilize the fleece by ironing Totally Stable to the wrong side of the fleece. Generally speaking, iron the stabilizer in place before transferring the design.

Transfer Method #1
Traced Solvy + Pins

1. Cut a piece of Sulky Solvy a little larger than the motif.

2. Make a design template by tracing the motif onto the Solvy with a permanent marking pen or fabric marker.

Advantages:
* Great for small to medium-sized motifs.
* Easy to trace designs.
* Great for adding details (leaf veins, eyelashes, tendrils).
* Solvy rinses away when finished.

Disadvantages:
* Awkward to handle for large motifs. (Choose one of the other transferring methods.)
* Since Solvy is only pinned in place, there is a tendency for the Solvy to "skootch" during stitching. Using a Teflon-coated presser foot reduces possible bunching.
* Not suitable for pintucked designs since the Solvy will act as a barrier, inhibiting the formation of a nice welt.

Additional Notes:
* If tracing with ink marker, make sure that the ink is permanent. The ink is permanent only on the surface on which it is drawn (the Solvy). When rinsed away, the ink rinses away with the Solvy rather than bleeding onto the fleece.
* If using a permanent pen to trace lines for sculpture stitching, I like to choose a color compatible with the thread color that will be stitched over it. That way, if the traced Solvy doesn't completely rinse out the first time, any trace ink lines will blend in with the stitching.

Transfer Method #2
Traced Solvy + KK2000 Temporary Adhesive Spray

Similar to Method #1, except the Solvy is temporarily adhered in place, rather than pinned in place. (Because we are using an adhesive, some of the rules change.)

1. Cut a piece of Sulky Solvy a little larger than the motif.

2. Make a design template by tracing the motif onto the Solvy, using a permanent marking pen or fabric marker.

3. Lightly spray KK2000 on the wrong side of the traced Solvy. (Spray only the Solvy, not the fleece.)

4. Adhere the traced Solvy to the fleece.

5. Peel off the Solvy after embellishing the motif. Do not rinse (KK2000 is not water-soluble).

Advantages:
* Great for small to medium-sized motifs that are simpler in design.
* Easy to trace designs.
* Great for adding details (leaf veins, eyelashes, tendrils).

Disadvantages:
* Awkward to handle for large motifs. (Choose one of the other transferring methods.)
* Tedious to remove Solvy if the design has a lot of intricate and close detail stitching. (Cannot rinse away when combined with KK2000 adhesive.)

Additional Note:
* If you need to stabilize the area with Totally Stable (for example, if you are doing sculpture stitching), iron the Totally Stable onto the wrong side of fleece before adhering the traced Solvy. If you iron fabric that has Solvy adhered with KK2000, the heat from the iron may interfere with the dissipation of the adhesive. Better safe than sorry.

Caution: Although the Solvy is water-soluble, the KK2000 is not. Do not attempt to rinse away the Solvy or you will end up with a gummy mess. Remove as much Solvy as possible. Most of the temporary adhesive will be removed with the Solvy, leaving only traces on the fleece. Allow the remaining adhesive to dissipate on its own (see Caution #3 on page 19).

Transfer Method #3
Traced Totally Stable + Stitch Transferring

Many times your design may be too large to easily trace onto water-soluble stabilizer. If your embellishment requires stabilized fleece, you can use Totally Stable iron-on tear-away stabilizer as the transfer medium.

1. Trace the design onto the "papery" or nonstick side of the Totally Stable.

2. Iron the traced Totally Stable onto the wrong side of the fleece, placing the design in the desired position.

3. To transfer the design to the right side of the fabric, straight stitch the entire motif from the wrong side of the fabric. For best visibility, use a longer stitch length and a bobbin thread slightly darker or lighter than the fleece color. Don't worry if the stitching isn't "pretty" – your embellishment will cover it. This stitching used as a guideline only.

4. From the right side of the fleece, embellish the motif using the just-stitched bobbin thread as a guide.

Advantages:

❋ Easy way to transfer large designs.

❋ Easy to combine pieces of Totally Stable for a very large motif.

❋ Best used for sculpturing, couching, fleece texturing, and embellishments that will cover the bobbin thread guideline stitching.

Disadvantages:

❋ Use only in those situations where you need stabilized fleece.

❋ Use only when the embellishing stitches will cover the bobbin guideline thread.

❋ For easiest tracing, use white Totally Stable.

Additional Note:

❋ Since you are stabilizing the fleece with the iron-on stabilizer, this technique is not suitable for pintucked designs. (The stabilization prevents welt formation. And the bobbin guideline thread would be visible.)

Caution: The finished motif will be reversed from the traced design. If the motif is a one-way design (rose with a side leaf, block-letter word, scroll, etc.), mirror image it before tracing it onto the Totally Stable.

Transfer Method #4
Mesh Transfer Canvas + Chacopel Pencils

You will love this delightful new product for transferring designs and motifs. You will find this an easy method for all your embellishing sewing (not just fleece!).

Mesh Transfer Canvas is a piece of fine gauge plastic mesh. It has the benefit of being reusable over and over again.

1. Lay the Mesh Transfer Canvas over the desired design and trace. You can trace the design onto the mesh transfer canvas using one of the following:

a. Lead pencil. Pro: Tracings easily wash away from the mesh, making it reusable. Con: The lines will be difficult to see if the traced mesh is overlaid onto darker colored fabric.

b. Clover Chacopel pencils. This is my personal favorite. These pencils easily mark the mesh and, because they come in three colors, are always visible against any color fabric. Tracings easily wash away from the mesh, making it reusable.

c. Permanent ink marker. Choose this if you want to make the mesh a permanent template for repetitive use. Quilters find this product handy for making quilt templates.

2. Lay the traced mesh canvas on your fleece and redraw the design using Clover Chacopel pencils, transferring the design onto the fleece. To transfer the design onto fleece, lay a single layer of fleece on a hard surface. For the pencil to mark easily, it needs the resistance of a hard surface like a table or countertop. If you mark on a double layer of fleece or on a padded ironing board, the fabric sinks as you draw the lines.

Need to reverse the design for right and left? Simply flip the mesh over to mirror image the design before transferring. This eliminates the need to use a light box or sunny window to draw mirror images, or the need to draw a right and left image.

Advantages:
* Extremely quick and easy to use.
* Easy to mirror image designs.
* Reusable over and over again. Remove traced design with soap and water.

Disadvantage:
* Does not work well on thick, deeply napped fleece.

Additional Notes:
* Sharpen the Chacopel pencils to a rounded medium point. If you overly sharpen, the points break off too easily.
* As noted above, work on a single layer of fleece on a hard surface when you draw on the fleece. You need the hard surface for resistance.
* This transfer method works well for any type of embellishing technique, from sculpturing to pin-tucking and everything in-between.

nancy's comment
Regardless of what you initially used to draw the design on the mesh, you want to use the Chacopel pencils to draw on the fleece. These pencils easily mark through the holes of the mesh.

Transfer Method #5
Golden Threads Quilting Paper: No-Marking Method

You can't get much easier than not marking at all! And here is a way to do exactly that. Originally developed for the quilting world, this alternative offers a no-hassle method for transferring designs.

The following techniques are reprinted with permission from Golden Threads, who advocate dropped feed dogs and free-motion quilting (because that's what this product was designed for). With their blessing, I have tailored the technique for "fleece purposes."

Single Motif

1. Choose a design and resize on a copy machine if necessary.

2. Use a pencil to trace the design onto the Quilting Paper.

3. Lightly spray KK2000 temporary adhesive spray on the wrong side of the traced motif and adhere to the fleece. (Spray the traced quilting paper, not the fleece.)

4. Stitch the motif, using whatever embellishment technique you have chosen.

5. Tear the traced Quilting Paper away and discard.

Multiple Motifs or Continuous Designs

This transferring method is the easiest way to make multiple copies of a motif. Whether you are going to use them individually or connect the motifs to create a continuous design, Quilting Paper makes the process a snap. (Continuous motifs are a great way to embellish jacket and vest fronts, edges, and hems.)

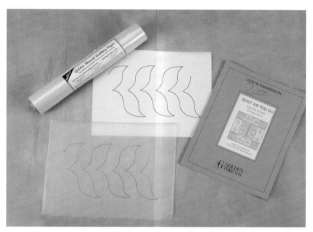

Motif from Golden Threads Strippy Quilt Pack.

1. Trace the design once onto Quilting Paper. (If using a continuous quilting template, trace one repeat. If making your own design, make sure the beginning and ending design lines of the motif will align with each other when used in repetition.)

2. For an easy way to make multiple copies, stack and pin together layers of Quilting Paper, having the traced design as the top layer. (Because this is a much lighter paper, a stack of 15 layers can be used.)

3. Lower the feed teeth.

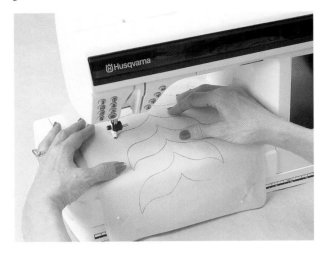

4. Insert a large needle (110/18 if you have one, 100/16 if you don't). The needle remains unthreaded. For bobbin sensor machines, leave a full bobbin in place. For machines with needle thread sensors, slip a business card into the tension area to trick the machine into thinking it is threaded.

5. Using free-motion quilting techniques, stitch through the stack of Quilting Paper, following the traced design. This creates a stack of perforated stitchable

stencils, which will be easy to follow when embellishing your fleece.

6. Lightly spray KK2000 on the wrong side of the design-perforated quilting paper and adhere to the fabric, matching the design lines for one continuous motif.

Troubleshooting: If your stitching tends to move the paper, if you are using a plastic presser foot, change to a metal foot. Lessen the pressure on your presser foot.

Advantages:
❋ Golden Threads Quilting Paper is much lighter weight than similar products. Because it is so sheer, it tears away cleanly without distorting stitches or leaving paper eyelashes to pick out. (Picking out tiny shreds of paper from stitching is not my idea of a fun time!)
❋ Unlike tissue paper, it is strong enough not to tear when stitching.
❋ It is a light golden color so it is easy to see on all fabric colors.
❋ It comes in 20-yard rolls, in widths of 12", 18", and 24", making it perfect for use with continuous designs.
❋ Ideal for sculpturing, couching, trapunto, appliqué, machine embroidery, duplicating designs.

Disadvantages:
❋ Not recommended for pintucking or branding (fleece texturizing) designs. Although Quilting Paper tears away cleanly, for the amount and type of stitching done in these techniques, that is demanding quite a lot.

Additional Notes:
❋ If your embellishment technique requires the fleece to be stabilized with Totally Stable (like sculpturing), iron the Totally Stable in place before adhering the stencil design with KK2000.
❋ Since this product is primarily used in the quilting world, look for it at your favorite local quilt shop.
❋ Golden Threads also offers a tremendous assortment of continuous line quilting design packs and templates that are wonderful for fleece embellishment.

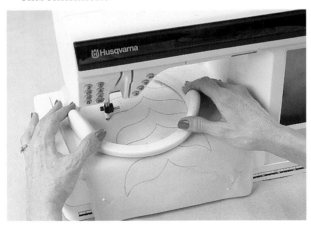

Uncomfortable with your level of expertise when it comes to free-motion stitching the multiple layers of Quilting Paper? Try using Quilt Sew Easy, that wonderful free-motion sewing tool featured on page 70.

Transfer Method #6
Flip & Draw

This is a simple way to transfer design lines for all types of embellishment. It is perfect for designs consisting of straight lines. This easy technique was introduced with Double Needle Sculpturing in *More Polarfleece® Adventures*.

1. Using pattern tracing material, trace the garment piece to be embellished.

2. Draw design lines for embellishment onto the pattern piece. (If garment has a two-piece front and the design is asymmetrical, match the right and left center fronts and pin them together. This allows for perfect alignment of design lines as they cross from the right to the left side.)

3. Cut the garment from fleece.

4. If the garment needs to be stabilized with Totally Stable for the embellishment technique chosen, stabilize the area before proceeding.

5. To draw design lines onto fleece garment:

a. Lay the fleece garment piece on a hard surface (table or countertop), right side up.

b. Lay the pattern piece with the drawn design lines on top of the fleece garment piece. The pattern piece should be right side up.

c. Lay a clear ruler on top of the pattern piece with the long edge exactly along a drawn design line.

d. Fold the pattern piece back over the ruler to expose the fleece. Use a Chacopel pencil to draw the design line onto the fleece.

e. Repeat until all the design lines are transferred onto the fleece.

Advantage:
❋ You can draw the design stitching lines directly onto your pattern piece, experimenting and playing with lines and proportions until you achieve exactly the balance you want. This is especially helpful when the design on the right and left fronts of a garment are asymmetrical.

Disadvantage:
❋ Since you are using the straight edge of the ruler as a guide, this only works with straight-line designs.

Important Notes Worth Repeating

* When using KK2000 temporary spray adhesive, always spray the adhesive onto whatever is being adhered to the fleece (stabilizer, paper, appliqué, etc.). *Never* spray directly onto the fleece.

* If your embellishment requires the fleece to be stabilized with Totally Stable, make that stabilization the first step of any transferring method you choose.

Chapter 4 ✳ Working With Border Prints

Nancy's Introductory Comments

During a conversation with David Cohen and Bert Levy, the owners of David Textiles, Inc. (a major fleece supplier to both the home sewing market and the manufacturing trade), I gave them a "wish list" of the types of print designs I wished I could find on fleece. They replied, "Why don't you design a fleece print collection for us?"

Excited at the prospect of having exactly what everyone was asking for, I started sketching ideas and putting colors together. Working with Beth Ann Bruske, the creative director for David Textiles, we produced a group of designs titled "Nancy's Collection," double border prints, nature-themed and scenic in flavor, reminiscent of the lush garments found in designer clothing. Many of the designs in this chapter are from that group. The base cloth has an anti-pill finish so it looks beautiful after wearing and laundering. Most important, these fleece prints are readily available at fabric stores across the nation!

Fleece border prints offer the home sewer a tremendous opportunity to copy the expensive designer looks found in better stores and specialty catalogs, and at the same time have some fun. Borders are not difficult to sew, but they do require a different thought process — you need to "think sideways."

Before we get into the different types of border prints, yardage calculations, and layout options, let's address the first question that automatically comes to mind: "What about the stretch?"

What About the Stretch?

Border prints are quite different from all-over prints. To take advantage of the print they require the garment pattern pieces to be laid out on the crossgrain rather than the traditional lengthwise straight-of-grain. Since fleece is a knit fabric, with the greater degree of stretch on the crossgrain, what happens when you lay out the pattern pieces on the opposite grain? How does that affect fit, wear, and pattern choice?

There are two important considerations to take into account. First, since fleece has 20% or more stretch on the crossgrain and little to moderate stretch on the lengthwise grain, laying the pattern pieces on the crossgrain removes most of the stretch factor from both the fit and the wearing ease of the garment. "Test stretch" your fabric before choosing a pattern. If your fleece has little or no stretch on the lengthwise grain, choose a pattern suitable for wovens. If your fleece has some lengthwise stretch, you may choose a pattern that requires "knits with moderate stretch" as long as it does not require a lot of stretch. (Avoid close-fitting patterns that require stretch for wearing ease.)

Second, choose a high quality fleece that has excellent memory and recovery. The stretch in a border print garment goes *up and down* the body rather than around the body. Fleece with poor memory or recovery will result in sagging bodies and pooched-out elbows. Before buying fabric, pre-test its memory. Give it a stretch in both directions and see how well it recovers. Higher quality fleece readily bounces back to its original dimension. Inferior fleece waves and ripples after the stretch test.

nancy's note

Many patterns are appropriate for use with either a knit (stretch) or woven (non-stretch) fabric. These patterns are not dependent upon the stretch of the fabric for fit or proper wearing ease, and are fine choices for use with border prints.

10" of fleece, on the fold, straight-of-grain, "relaxed."

10" of fleece stretched to 11", showing 10% stretch factor.

10" of fleece, on the fold, crossgrain, "relaxed."

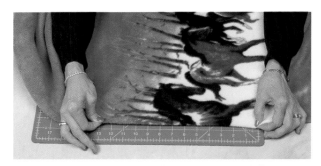

10" of fleece stretched to 13", showing 30% stretch factor.

Border Types & Yardage Calculations

You will find three types of border arrangements: Even Double Border, Uneven Double Border, and Single Border.

It is important to determine what kind of border print you have before calculating yardage needs. The pattern layouts vary according to the type of border print, and the yardage requirements are different. It's not difficult. It's quite logical. Just remember to "think sideways."

The basic premise is that instead of using the traditional pattern layout requirements geared around body length plus sleeve length for yardage calculations, *border print yardage needs are determined by body width and sleeve width.*

nancy's hint

If after reading the specifics about the different borders below you just want a quick and easy way to estimate the yardage needs, see "Yardage Guesstimate" on page 37.

Even Double Border Prints

The Even Double Border print is the most common and most desirable print because it is by far the easiest to work with and requires the least yardage. Because the identical print runs parallel to and equidistant from 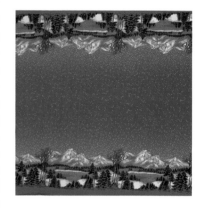 both selvages, you have the freedom to lay pattern pieces along either selvage edge.

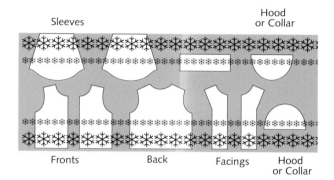

Sleeves — Hood or Collar

Fronts — Back — Facings — Hood or Collar

Calculating Yardage for Even Double Border Prints

To estimate yardage needs for an Even Double Border, calculate the *hemline* needs by adding widths across both garment fronts, back and front facings (if applicable). If the garment has a hood, add half the hood front edge length.

As you can see in the illustration, you need to calculate only the body widths because the sleeves lay out opposite the body pieces. Yardage for the garment fronts and back more than account for the sleeve needs, however hoods and/or facing needs must be added.

nancy's hint

When adding for facings (cut-on or sewn-on), measure across the widest part of the facings to figure yardage needs.

Uneven Double Border Prints

The Uneven Double Border print features the print parallel to both selvages, but the print design is placed at different distances away from each selvage edge. Or, you may find that the print designs differ on

the opposite selvages. The print design at one selvage may be a smaller version or a pullout version of the print design on the opposite edge.

If the design is the same at both selvages but just set at different distances from the selvage, the manufacturer did this for efficient fabric usage in layout. In ready-to-wear garment production, all the garment fronts and backs are placed along the selvage with the print design set furthest away (so that the design is featured above the hem or across the chest). The print set closest to the selvage is used for the sleeves (so the design accents the hem).

If the Uneven Double Border print has a smaller or pullout version at one edge, it was designed so the sleeve hems and hood edges coordinate with the garment hem edge but are just a bit different in

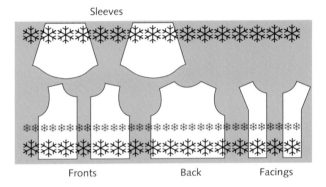

Sleeves

Fronts   Back   Facings

scale or design to create higher interest.

Calculating Yardage for Uneven Double Border Prints

The Uneven Double Border may take a little bit more yardage since you are restricted as to where you will place individual pattern pieces. You have to plan which selvage edge will be used for collars, hoods, and facings. The illustration shows the typical placement for garment pieces using an uneven print.

Single Border Prints

Single Border prints are not as common as Double Border prints. A Single Border print runs parallel to one selvage only and the

rest of the fabric is a uniform color or all-over print.

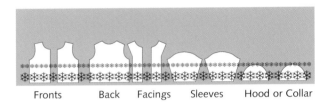

Fronts   Back   Facings   Sleeves   Hood or Collar

Calculating Yardage for Single Border Prints

The Single Border print takes the most yardage because you only have the design along one selvage. This means you will need to calculate yardage by adding up all the "widths" of the pattern pieces that will feature the design.

When using a Single Border print, it is common for the border to be featured on the garment fronts and back, while the sleeves and collar are cut from the solid area.

Yardage Requirements Recap

If you have a specific garment pattern in mind, here's how to calculate the necessary yardage for an **Even Double Border print**. Add elements #1, #2, #3, and #4 together as they apply to your garment.

1. Total circumference of jacket including seam allowances and widest part of cut-on facing, if applicable. (Left Front + Right Front + Back)

2. Both front facings, across the widest part. (If garment has separate facings.)

3. One collar length. (No need to add collar length if there are front facings since they will lay out opposite each other.)

4. Half the hood height, if your garment has a hood. (The other half lays out on the opposite selvage.)

The garment fronts and back are placed along one selvage while the sleeves are laid out at the opposite selvage. (That's why there is no yardage calculation for the sleeves.) If you have front facings, a collar can be laid out opposite the facings. If you have a hood where you want the border design to frame your face, cut half the hood at one border and the other half at the opposite border.

Additional Consideration

If there is a definite design repeat (one distinctive tree, a noticeable bear in the woods, a flock of birds in the sky, a geometric motif, etc.), add one design repeat to your calculated yardage needs. This additional repeat allows a little grace room for balancing center fronts, matching sleeves, placing a specific design on a collar, etc.

Yardage Guess-timate

Nancy's "Cheater's Way" to Figure Yardage Requirements

This approach is especially helpful when you fall madly in love with an Even Double Border print but haven't chosen a specific pattern. You can quite accurately "guess-timate" how much fleece you'll need as follows:

Jacket Guess-timate

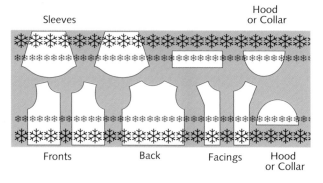

1. Take your personal hip measurement and add 14". (This accounts for moderate wearing ease and seam allowances, and assumes the sleeves are laid out at the opposite border.)

2. Add 1/2 yard for a collar or front facings (separate or cut-on). If you want both facings and a collar, only add the 1/2 yard once.

3. Add 1/2 yard for a hood.

4. Add one "design repeat" if your border has a definite repeat.

These calculations generally work out to be a minimum of 2 yards or a little more for a simple, basic jacket. (Which is amazingly close to traditional yardage requirements stated on pattern envelopes!) I usually add 1/4 yard for good measure because I'd rather have 9" too much than 5" too little! This is my absolute minimum amount to buy. Safer yet is 2-1/2 yards, and 3 yards offers lots of breathing room and more pattern choices. (Plus there are always great uses for leftovers!)

Vest Guess-timate

1. Take your personal hip measurement and add 14". Divide by 2. (Since you will lay the front pieces along one selvage and the back piece along the opposite selvage, you only need half the garment total hem width.)

2. Add 1/2 yard for a collar or front facings if applicable. If you want both facings and collar, add the 1/2 yard only once. (They will lay out opposite each other.)

3. Add 1/2 yard for a hood.

4. Add one "design repeat" if your border has a definite repeat.

This works out to be about 3/4 yard to 1 yard for a simple vest, or 1-1/4 to 1-1/2 yards for a collared or hooded vest.

If you want a longer tunic length vest, lay out the fronts and back on the same border edge and calculate the yardage accordingly. (Hip measurement plus 14". Add 1/2 yard for collar or facings.)

nancy's caution

The finished length of a vest must be 26" or less to lay out the fronts and back opposite each other. (Half the fabric width is 30", but you need to allow room for hems and shoulder height.)

Traditional border layout with border accent at the hemline.

Traditional Layout

This positioning of the garment pieces highlights the border design at the hemline of the garment and the sleeves.

Lay the front, back, and sleeve pattern pieces with the hems towards the selvage edge.

If your border is an uneven one, touching garment pieces (fronts and back and facings) or matching pieces (sleeves or both hood halves) must be laid out at the same selvage.

Traditional border layout with border accent at the hemline.

Untraditional border layout with border accent across shoulders to frame the face.

Untraditional Layout

This positioning highlights the border design across the shoulder, bust, and upper arm, focusing attention to your face.

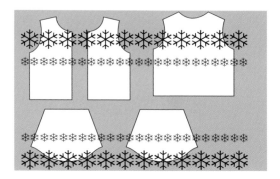

Lay the front, back, and sleeve pattern pieces with the neck/shoulder edge and the sleeve cap towards the selvage edge and the hems towards the midpoint of the fleece.

Of course, the print must be appropriate. The Falling Leaves and the Snowflake border prints are perfect examples of borders that can take advantage of the both the traditional and untraditional layouts. Obviously, forests and landscape scenes do not offer the same versatility. Somehow the charm is lost when trees and mountains are upside down!

Things to Consider

1. Before beginning to cut, completely lay out your pattern fronts, back, sleeves, facings, and hood or collar to allocate space properly. (This is a good time to take heed of the old home improvement adage "Measure twice, cut once.")

2. Don't forget hem allowances when placing the pattern pieces along the selvage. It's easy to get sidetracked by the drama of the border print and forget to take into account that there are likely to be a couple inches involved in a hem allowance.

3. To match the design on the garment body to the design on the sleeve, position the armscye points of the fronts and back and the underarm points of the sleeve at the same place in the print design. (Refer to the illustrations.)

4. If your print has a distinctive motif repeat (a noticeable tree, a stately bear, a mountain peak), position that distinctive part of the design decid-

edly off-center on both the front and the back of the garment. First and foremost, it is visually more pleasing this way. Secondly, you avoid the risk of a design looking as though it were not quite centered properly. If the print has a *close* repetitive design, center a motif on the front, back, and each sleeve.

5. Depending on the garment pattern chosen and the design of the fleece, you may need to lengthen or shorten a pattern piece a little to place the border design exactly where you want it.

6. Want a longer jacket? If your print design allows, you may lengthen the garment body by

"encroaching" past the midway point and onto the "sleeve half" of the fleece. Sleeves do not need their 30" allotment.

No-Side-Seam Jacket or Vest Layout

This clever technique was shown in *Adventures With Polarfleece®*. The technique provides a lovely continuous border without the interruption of side seams. Suitable for both jackets and vests, it is necessary to use a pattern with relatively straight side seams and no side seam pockets or side seam detailing. (If pockets are desired, create welt or patch pockets.)

The jacket or vest can have a straight or shaped bottom edge and can be laid out using the traditional or untraditional layout.

How to Eliminate the Side Seams

1. Overlap the front and back jacket or vest pattern pieces at the side seam underarm points, 2 times the seam allowance. (Overlap 1-1/4" if the pattern has a 5/8" seam allowance. Overlap 1/2" if the pattern has a 1/4" seam allowance.)

2. Adjust the amount of overlap at the side seam bottom edge of the garment pattern pieces so that the center back fold line is parallel to the front straight-of-grain lines. (The amount of overlap may be less at the bottom edge than at the underarm edge.)

3. Cut out the jacket or vest in one piece.

Choosing a Pattern

As explained previously, choose a pattern with minimal or no stretch requirements.

Because the drama of the garment will be in the uniqueness of the border print, choose a pattern with simple lines that won't interfere with the print design. Avoid lots of seamlines and details. Avoid cut-up or blocked areas. Simple fronts, back, and one-piece sleeves work best. A yoked garment can work but it takes a bit more planning, thinking, and yardage calculation.

Eliminate patch pockets. Replace them with side seam pockets or unobtrusive zipped welt pockets.

Generally speaking, for the most efficient use of fabric yardage, plan for the garment pieces to fit in "half a border." Basically you have 30" working space, half the fabric width, for garment fronts and back, and the other 30" for sleeves. Choose a jacket or top that has a finished body length of 26" or less, or one that can be shortened a couple inches, if necessary, to fit the print. As discussed earlier, if your print allows, you can encroach a few inches across the halfway point for a slightly longer body length. However, if you want a coat length, the yardage needs will be significantly greater, comparable to a Single Border print.

Sewing Tips for Border Prints

Sewing techniques are the same as outlined in Chapter 1– A Quick Refresher Course, with these additional considerations:

1. Since you are working with a border design, the garment pieces are cut out on the crossgrain. That means the greatest degree of stretch will be running up and down center front and up and down the side seams.

2. Lengthen the stitch length to 4mm to prevent waving when sewing the center front or side seams. If using a serger, "plus," or increase, the differential setting when sewing the side seams to prevent waving or rippling. (Test on a scrap to determine how much to "plus.")

3. To prevent stretching in a garment with a side seam pocket opening, include a strip of stabilizer or seam tape along the fold, or clear elastic in the seam.

4. When applying a zipper, be sure to use a wash-away stitch-through basting tape and a long (4mm) stitch length to prevent buckling.

5. When sewing a knit layer to a woven layer, as when adding a woven lining to a fleece garment, place the fleece (stretch) fabric against the feed dogs and the woven (nonstretch) fabric facing up. This arrangement allows you to hold the woven layer taut and take advantage of the movement of the feed dogs to help ease the knit into the seam. (If the knit layer was on top, the pressure from the presser foot would stretch the fleece, making the seamline uneven.)

Chapter 5

*P*OLAR RIBBING REVISITED

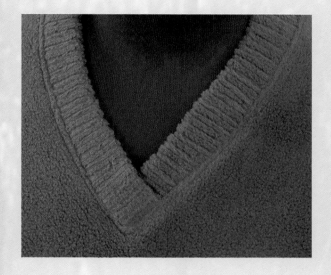

Polar ribbing is an exciting technique that you'll use again and again. It was the runaway favorite technique featured in *More Polarfleece® Adventures*. The simple use of double needle pintucking to make fabric "look like ribbing" opens up a whole new world of professional looking garment finishes. Now you can make "ribbing" to match all your garments!

This technique works on a wide variety of fabrics, not just fleece. It is especially wonderful for fleece because it is virtually impossible to find matching rib for fleece. The colors of cotton-blend ribbing look flat against the color depth of polyester fleece. Nylon ribbing offers great color strength but tends to feel rough against the skin when used on indoor garments.

10" of fleece, on the fold, on the crossgrain, "relaxed."

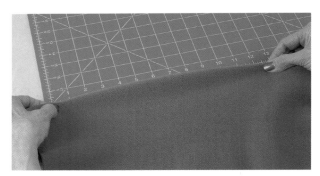

10" of fleece, stretched to 12-1/2", showing 25% stretch factor.

The criteria for determining if a fabric is suitable for making ribbing is that it must have sufficient stretch to use for self-fabric bands and cuffs. While the criteria for many other techniques in this book is for the fabric to have loft (to create texture with stitching), the criteria for making polar ribbing is stretch.

The directions on the back of many pattern envelopes state, "You may use self-fabric for cuffs, bands, and neck trim if your fabric has at least 25% stretch." Or it may picture an arrow and state, "You may use self-fabric for trim if your fabric stretches

from here to here." In other words, the fleece needs a bit of stretch so the cuffs will slip over the hand and hug the wrist, so the bottom band will hug the hips, so the neckband will fit over the head without gaping at the neck.

Please read all the rules and information below before you begin to make ribbing. There are many simple hints that will make your rib experience easier, sidestep any potential difficulties, and eliminate problems before they happen. Five minutes of reading now will, in the long run, save you lots of time and produce better results.

Polar Ribbing Rules

Polar Ribbing Rule #1

Fleece must have enough stretch to be suitable for self-fabric trim.

nancy's note

Most fleeces have a nice amount of stretch on the crossgrain. However, there are a few fleeces that have virtually no stretch. Those fleeces won't work for this idea. When in doubt, hold a strip of fleece around your wrist and see if it has enough stretch to allow you to slip your hand through. How it fits now is how it will fit when it becomes ribbing. You are not making the fleece act like ribbing; you are just making it look like ribbing!

Polar Ribbing Rule #2

Pintucks are always sewn on the straight-of-grain (in the direction of least stretch).

Polar Ribbing Rule #3

Always, always, always test sew a sample of pintucking rows.

A test sampler allows you to see if you like the thread choice, the size of the welts, the spacing of the welts, and to check the nap of the fabric.

Thread Choice

Use good quality, long staple polyester thread in a matching color. Contrasting thread is also a option as it lends a very subtle delineation to the rib welts. Rayon or metallic thread may be used, but test first to make sure the special qualities of these threads aren't lost in the loft of the fabric. Always use regular thread in the bobbin.

Double Needles

Double needle sizes are expressed in two numbers, i.e. 2.5/80, 4.0/90, and 6.0/100. The decimal number indicates the space, in millimeters, between the needles. The whole number refers to the size of the needles. The needle package also lists a designation as to the needle type (stretch, metallic, embroidery). If no type is listed, it is normally a universal needle.

Double Needle Width = Size of "Ribs"

The size of the ribs, or welts, formed by the double needles is determined by the amount of space between the needles. Smaller numbers (narrower needle separation) like 1.6 and 2.0 produce the tiny welts used in delicate heirloom sewing. Sizes 2.5, 3.0, 4.0, 6.0, and 8.0 produce progressively larger welts and are used on medium to heavier fabrics, for topstitching, hemming, decorative texturizing effects, and for our purposes… polar ribbing. Sizes 3.0, 4.0, and 6.0 double needles are the preferred choice for fleece ribbing, with 4.0 and 6.0 being the most popular. (Before choosing a 6.0 double needle, refer to your sewing machine manual to make sure your machine will accommodate this size.)

A 4.0 double needle offers a nice, medium-sized welt for a moderate ribbed look. A 6.0 double needle provides a coarse, dramatic, sporty-looking ribbing. Some older machines may not be able to use double needles wider than 3.0, which result in a finer ribbed look. Choose the needle separation according to the thickness of your fleece and the capability of your machine.

3.0 double needle results in "fine" ribs.

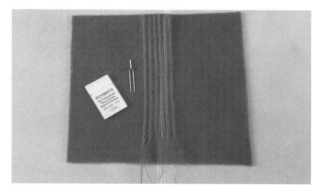

4.0 double needle results in "medium" ribs.

6.0 double needle results in "coarse" sporty ribs.

Double Needle Size

Just like using regular single needles, choose the needle size to fit the fabric weight. The smaller the number, the finer or smaller the needle. The larger the number, the larger and stronger the needle shaft. Since most fleeces you will be "ribbing" are in the mid-weight category, choose a 75/11, 80/12, 90/14, or 100/16 size designation. You will notice that the wider double needles correspond to larger size needles for more strength and less deflection.

nancy's note

The 80/12 size is a dual number showing the European/U.S. size designation. Double needles only refer to the European number when designating the size. So a 3.0/80 needle size would be an 80/12. (You can only get so many numbers on a small needle package, so the U.S. number had to go!)

Double Needle Type

Remember my famous rule from the Refresher Chapter: "If the conditions change, the rules change." Since fleece is a knit fabric, the general needle type used would be a standard universal or stretch (ballpoint) double needle when pintucking with regular thread.

If you pintuck with rayon thread, use an embroidery needle. (An embroidery double needle has a universal point but offers a larger eye and deeper groove to better accommodate the larger dimension of the rayon thread.)

If you choose to pintuck with metallic thread, use a metallic or embroidery double needle. (The larger eye and deeper groove configuration allows the rougher metallic thread to flow smoothly with less shredding or thread breakage. For best results with metallic thread, use a size 90.)

If there is no specification on the needle package as to its type, it is a standard universal needle.

Figuring "Yardage"

Not real yardage in the traditional sense, but you do need to know how much additional fabric to purchase for ribbing.

Since fleece is 60" wide, figure one cut for the bottom band, and one cut for neck trim and cuffs. In theory, if the pattern calls for 6" bands and cuffs, you would need two 6" strips and would purchase 1/3 yard extra to make polar ribbing trim. However, I would buy 1/2 yard, for the reason explained below.

If your pattern calls for a 6" strip of ribbing or self-fabric to be folded in half for a finished band, and you are going to make a polar ribbing band,

nancy's hints

Rather than cutting the exact called-for width in your pattern directions, by beginning with a wider-than-necessary strip, you stand a better chance of sewing attractive ribs.

make life easier on yourself and start out with an 8" wide strip of fleece. That way, if perhaps your beginnings and endings aren't quite as precise as you'd like them to be, you will always have a good 6" in the middle to work with. In other words, make your strip 2" wider than you really need. (It's insurance. If you bunch up or get offgrain at the edges, it doesn't make any difference because you are pintucking more width than you actually need and will use only the center area.)

Spacing the Ribs

Ribbing shown: Presser foot width spacing, every-other-groove, and side-by-side ribs.

For distinctive and realistic ribbing, the most popular spacing of pintuck welts is every-other-groove (with a 3.0 needle and a five-groove presser foot) or using the 4.0 or 6.0 double needle and aligning the outer edge of the presser foot against each welt as you sew the new row. This spacing can be fine tuned to exactly the look you want by moving the needle position from center towards the left. When moving the needle position to the left, realize that you are moving two needles. This means you will not be able to move to the far left needle position (or you will break one of the needles!).

Avoid side-by-side ribs. This snug spacing of welts exactly next to each other greatly reduces the stretch. (Besides, it would take forever to sew!)

Stitch Length

Sew with a 3.0mm stitch length. There is no need to backtack or tie off the beginning and ending stitches. The pintuck ends will be secured when sewn to the garment.

The "Nap Effect"

Test sewing is a must every time you make polar ribbing. You absolutely need to do a test run to determine in which direction you will sew the rows of pintucks. Every fleece reacts differently. The depth of color and the height of the nap greatly affect your decision.

1. Place a sample cut of fleece on your machine, right side up. (When tugging on the crossgrain, fleece curls to the wrong side.)

2. Sew the first set of test pintucks on the straight-of-grain (the direction of least stretch), beginning all rows at the same edge.

3. Skip 1" or 2" and sew 6 to 8 pintuck rows, beginning all the rows at the opposite edge of the fleece strip (changing the direction of nap).

4. Skip 1" or 2" and sew 6 to 8 pintucks rows, sewing back-and-forth (with the nap, against the nap, with the nap, against the nap, etc.).

This pintuck testing will show whether the nap affects the direction in which you will want to stitch the pintucks welts. Your test will produce one of the following results:

Ribbing shown: "With the nap" and "against the nap."

1. One set of pintucks looks clean and crisp (sewn with the nap). Another set looks rough and scruffy, like petting a cat backwards (against the nap). The third set looks messy (clean, scruffy, clean, scruffy, etc.). In this scenario, you would choose to sew all the pintucks "with the nap" for a crisp ribbing with distinctive welts.

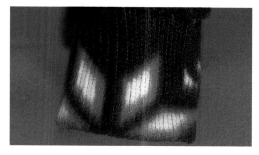

2. The pintucks show no discernible difference when you sew with the nap, against the nap, or up-down, up-down. This means you can sew the pintuck welts any direction you want and the look will be consistent.

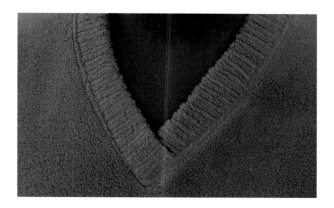

3. The pintucks react the same as in #1, except instead of looking messy, the "clean, scruffy, clean, scruffy" effect looks like rich luscious chenille.

Bottom line: You don't know how the pintucks will look until you test the nap and see what looks best. Take the five minutes. It is definitely worth it!

How to Make Polar Ribbing

You've done your homework by making a test sample. You've determined what width double needles to use, checked the nap and determined which direction to sew the pintucks, and determined the spacing of the ribs. Now it's time for the grand finale.

1. Before beginning sewing, wind extra bobbins with regular thread.

nancy's hint

Since the bobbin thread won't be visible, this is a good opportunity to use up all those pesky leftover partial spools of thread cluttering up your sewing area. Just make sure they aren't old or weak.

2. Insert the double needle and attach the appropriate presser foot.

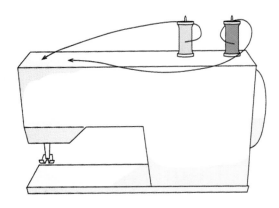

3. Using two spools of regular thread, thread the machine and both needles.

a. If you have two vertical spool holders on the back of your machine, place the spools so they feed off the spools in opposite directions. One thread feeds off the back of the spool, the other thread feeds off the front. This arrangement keeps the threads away from each other and prevents tangling.

b. If you have a horizontal spool holder on your machine, your machine should also have available a vertical spool holder attachment for the second spool.

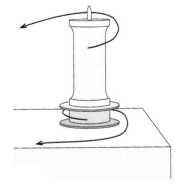

c. If you only have one vertical spool holder, place a filled bobbin on the bottom of the spool holder, topping it with your spool of thread. Arrange the bobbin and the spool of thread so they rotate in opposite directions as the thread is being pulled off. This arrangement helps prevent thread tangling.

d. When threading your machine for double needle stitching, separate the threads every time you have the opportunity. Place one thread on the left side of the tension disc and the other thread on the right side of the tension disc. If you have two thread guides going into the needle, use one thread in each guide. If you only have one thread guide before the needles, you may find that your machine sews better if one thread is in the guide and the other thread bypasses the guide. Test sew to check.

e. Refer to your sewing machine manual for double needle threading guidelines specific to your machine.

4. Cut strips of fleece 60" x 8" (or whatever width you need for the rib trim you are making). Greater degree of stretch is going in the 60" length.

5. To estimate the quantity of fleece you need to pintuck, use the first 10" you pintuck as a "rib gauge."

a. Determine the right side of the fleece. (When tugging on the long cut edge of fleece, it will curl to the wrong side.)

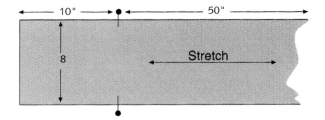

b. On the right side of the fleece, use pins or a fabric marker to mark 10" from one end.

c. Sew pintuck rows to fill the marked 10" section.

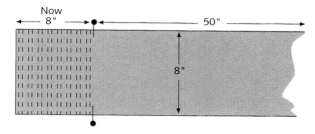

d. Measure the 10" "rib gauge" section and compare the measurements before and after pintucking.

For example, if the original 10" has "shrunk" to 8" (having been drawn up by the multiple rows of pintucks), it means that 20% of the original length was lost to pintucking. Use this information to figure approximately how much fleece length to pintuck to net out the length you need for neckband, collar, cuffs, or bottom bands.

Additional Consideration: If there is a print motif that you want centered on a cuff or collar, make sure to allow for it.

6. Pintuck as much fleece as necessary for your garment trim finish. There is no need to backtack or tie off the beginning and ending stitches since the finished rib will be cut to size later.

nancy's hint

Keep the straight and narrow. After sewing row upon row of pintuck welts, it's easy to start getting off kilter, with the rows starting to tilt at an angle. If you see that happening, gradually correct the rows as you sew to get back on the straight and narrow.

Continuous Rib: Quick-Sew Ribbing

There are only so many ways of doing things in this world. Who says you can't reinvent the wheel? Much innovative sewing comes from using old techniques in new ways. Thanks for this clever, useful, and timesaving technique goes to Jean Libbey, owner of The Sewing Network, a Viking/Pfaff sewing machine dealership in Auburn, Maine. Jean offered this brilliant new application of an old idea while I was teaching Polar Ribbing at a Husqvarna Viking Convention.

Remember the technique for making continuous bias binding? It's that clever technique where you butt and sew the edges of fabric together so that you can cut in one long continuous strip? The general premise is the same. Instead of continuous cutting, you will do continuous pintucking!

1. Remove the sewing table from your sewing machine to expose the free arm.

2. Use a tape measure to measure the circumference of the free arm and add 2".

3. Cut a strip of fleece to make Polar Ribbing as follows: Instead of cutting a fleece strip the width you actually need, cut it the circumference of the free arm plus 2" wide. (If your free arm circumference is 10", cut your fleece 12" wide). Cut the length you need plus anticipated shrinkage from pintucking.

4. Insert a double needle and attach the appropriate presser foot to your machine.

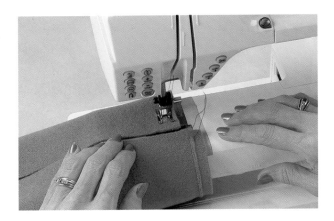

5. Place the fleece under the presser foot, right side up. Sew the first pintuck one presser foot width away from the cut edge, sewing on the straight-of-grain. Stop and sink the needles into the fleece (to hold it in place) just before you get to the end of the first row.

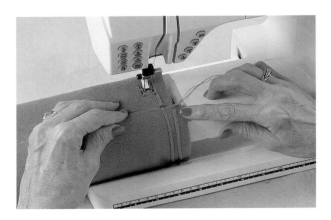

6. Bring the beginning of the just-sewn pintuck row under the free arm (from the back of the machine, under the free arm towards the front). Butt the beginning edge of the fleece to the ending edge of the fleece, offsetting the pintucked row by the spacing you have chosen for your ribs. (In the photo, the ribs are sewn a presser foot width apart.)

7. Continue sewing across the butted edge, immediately resulting in the beginning of the second row. (You are now sewing in a circle, or "what goes around, comes around.")

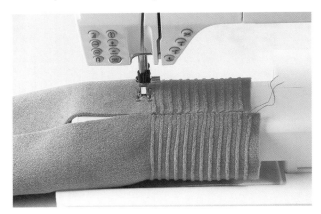

8. Continue sewing "in a circle" until the entire strip is pintucked. Be careful to keep the pintuck rows even and straight. (Just because it is fast and easy, don't be lured into a "pedal to the metal" mindset. Pay attention to sewing accurate pintuck rows.)

9. Cut the "sew across" threads at the butted edges.

10. Cut the Polar Ribbing into collars, cuffs, or bottom band.

Important Polar Ribbing Information

❋ Remember, it just looks like ribbing, it doesn't act like ribbing. Keep that in mind when you are sewing it to your garment.

❋ The first step of the cuff (or ribbed band) construction is to sew the cuff into a circle so you can apply it to the sleeve edge. Use a conventional sewing machine for this step, and finger press the seam allowance open. (A serged seam would be too bulky.)

❋ Don't stretch the "polar rib" when sewing it to the garment. The beginning and ending stitches are not secure until they are sewn into the garment and can easily pull out.

❋ To compensate for less stretch in Polar Ribbing (remember, it's not really ribbing), run two rows of gathering stitches along the lower edge of the sleeve and the lower edge of the garment. Gather the garment to be slightly larger than the Polar Ribbing cuff or bottom band dimension. Sew the ribbing to the garment using a 3.0mm stitch length. (A serger is great for this step, especially when using the differential feed to ease the garment into the ribbing.) Remove the gathering stitches.

❋ Since Polar Ribbing doesn't have as much stretch or recovery as real ribbing, adjust the length of ribbing used for cuffs and bottom band as follows:

a. Cuffs: Fold the Polar Ribbing in half lengthwise and cut it long enough to comfortably slip your hand through. Add 1/2" for the seam allowance. If using a printed fleece, plan for centering a motif.

b. Bottom band: Fold the Polar Ribbing in half lengthwise and hold it around your hip area for a comfortable fit. Add 1/2" for the seam allowance. If using a print fleece, plan for centering a motif at the center front.

c. Pull-on neckband trim: Fold the Polar Ribbing in half lengthwise and pinch with your fingers at the length suggested by the pattern. Hold it in a circle around your head and lengthen just as much as is necessary to be able to slip your head through. Remember that Polar Ribbing doesn't have the stretch or recovery of real ribbing. Unless your fleece is lightweight and very stretchy, avoid turtlenecks. Narrower trim works best. Polar Ribbed v-necks and collars are always safe.

Besides the practical and everyday use of Polar Ribbing, pintucking is a fabulous technique to use for subtly texturizing fleece. Refer to *More Polarfleece® Adventures* for lots of ideas, techniques, and embellishment information.

The last word, one last time… Polar Ribbing just *looks* like ribbing. It does not *act* like ribbing.

Chapter 6 NEW EDGE FINISHES

Garment finishing details offer fertile ground for sewers to express their individuality and add personality to their fleece garments. Fleece characteristics allow for a wide range of experimentation with unique effects. In Chapter 5 you took advantage of the stretch and loft of fleece to make your own Polar Ribbing. In this chapter, you'll explore other possibilities.

"Make-Your-Own-Border" Edge Finish

Combine a print fleece with a solid color fleece, frame the garment with a "created border," finish with Polar Ribbing, and you'll have a ready-to-wear designer look. Best of all… it's easy!

With so many gorgeous fleece all-over prints to choose from, you can easily design your own border print garments. Choose a print with a motif that offers some sort of band, stripe, or repetitive print that can be cut into strips and used to accent hems, zippers, hood edges, pocket edges, and sleeve hems.

For easy sewing and a crisp look, choose a fleece that has a clean blunt edge when cut with a rotary cutter.

This technique is not appropriate for Berber or plush fabrics.

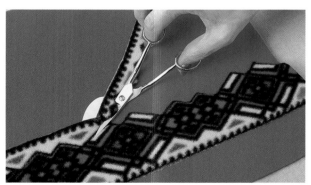

Another option: Cut the print to make a shaped-edge border.

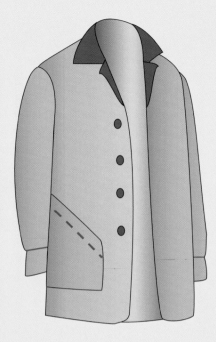
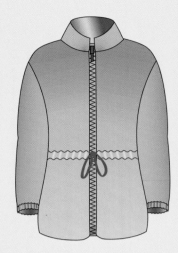

Choose a garment pattern that offers appropriate lines for border accents. The garment needs to have straight edges to lay the border along. Zipped front. Straight bottom edge. Straight hemmed sleeve. Stand-up collar. Hood. Patch pocket. You don't want all of these elements, but you do want enough of them to make a statement. Don't forget, you can add some details of your own like shoulder epaulets or an outside casing at the waistline for a draw cord.

This garment offered lots of options. It was just a matter of picking how much accent was desired, and where to put the accent.

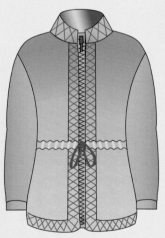

Border accent: Collar, center front, and hem.

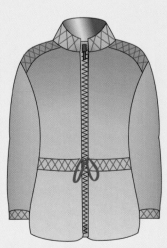

Border accent: Collar, shoulder, waist, and sleeve hem.

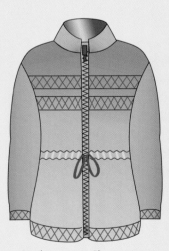

Border accent: Chest stripes, garment and sleeve hems.

Border Example

Borders can have a straight or shaped edge. Follow the print design or create your own edge shape. You can trim the border edge to its finished edge/shape either before or after sewing it in place.

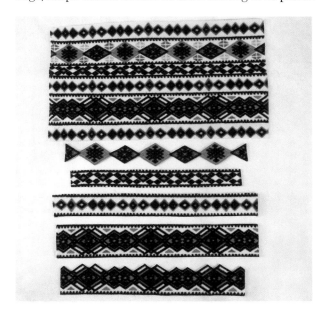

Cutting Border Strips

Cutting the Border Edge After Application

1. Cut the border strip 1" or so wider than the finished edge will be. After adhering it in position, straight stitch the border edge, following a print line for direction. Peel back the excess border edge and trim close to the stitching line. Appliqué or embroidery scissors will give the neatest cut.

Cutting the Finished Border Edge Before Application

1. Using a rotary cutter or sharp scissors, cut the edge of the border to its finished look and dimension, leaving a clean blunt edge. Use an edgestitch or edge guide presser foot and move the needle to the left needle position to edgestitch the border in place.

Applying Borders

This is the general approach to applying border trim to various portions of a garment. Adapt as necessary to be compatible with your pattern's specific construction directions.

Garment/Sleeve, Hem/Hood
Pretend you are facing a hem, except that you are working from the inside out.

1. Cut the garment to the finished body length. Trim away the hem allowance.

2. Cut the border strip, allowing 1/4" extra for a hem seam allowance along one long edge. Cut the border strip the length necessary to fit the garment hem or sleeve hem. When cutting the border length, allow for motif placement at the center front or center of the sleeve.

3. Pin the right side of the border strip against the wrong side of the garment, with the raw edges even. Sew with a 1/4" seam allowance, using a 4.0mm stitch length.

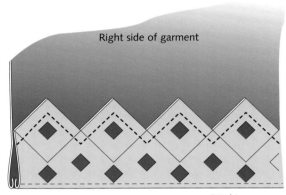
Right side of garment

Stitching

4. Turn the border to the right side of the garment, rolling the seam allowance slightly to the underside. Pin in position, placing the pins parallel to and close to the bottom edge of the hem (at the just-sewn seam).

5. Peel the border strip back and lightly spray KK2000 temporary adhesive spray on the border. Finger press to adhere in place. (*Note:* Spray only the wrong side of the border strip. Do not spray the fleece garment.)

6. Stitch the border in place.

nancy's note

Since this seam is sewn on the cross-grain, in the direction of most stretch, the longer stitch length will prevent a wavy seam.

Stand-Up Collar

1. Alter the pattern width if necessary to accommodate the border print. Construct the collar following the pattern directions.

Patch Pockets
The patch pocket treatment is similar to the garment hem.

1. Trim the cut-on pocket facing or seam allowance to produce a pocket of the finished height.

2. Apply the border strip the same as the garment hem.

3. Sew the patch pocket to the garment, using the blunt edge technique.

a. Using a rotary cutter, cut the outer edges of the pocket to the finished dimension.

b. Apply Wash-Away basting tape to the wrong side of the pocket along the outer edges and tape in place.

c. Edgestitch, then topstitch the pocket in place, leaving the raw pocket edges exposed.

Zippers

1. Eliminate front facings and/or lining if the garment has them.

2. Sandwich the zipper between the border and the garment body front. (When following the pattern directions, pretend the border strip is the garment front and treat your garment front as though it were the facing or lining. When reading the pattern directions, replace "front" with "border strip" and replace "lining or facing" with "front." The end result will be a zipper sandwiched between the border strip and garment front.)

Faux Epaulets

1. Sew the fronts to the back at the shoulder seam.

2. Lightly spray the wrong side of the border strip and adhere it on top of the shoulder seamline.

3. Trim the border strips even with the neck edge and armhole edge.

4. Edgestitch the border in place.

5. Proceed with the collar and sleeve application.

Inside-Out Wrapped Edges

This technique is similar to making your own border print, except that instead of using a printed design for a border, you will create your own dramatic shaped edge from a contrast solid fleece, for a great positive/negative effect.

This idea is best suited to plain-front jackets and vests without collars or lapels, and straight hemmed sleeves. For purposes of illustration, I show a vest front. The same directions apply to the back or sleeve.

I call the shaped edge an "outside facing" because, in essence, that is what it is. It is a facing that you are using on the outside of the garment.

1. Using pattern tracing material, trace the garment front, back, sleeves, etc.

a. Trace the front and hem edges to the finished length.

b. Eliminate any cut-on facings.

2. Using the traced pattern pieces as the base, draw a 1-1/2" to 6" wide "outside facing." It may be larger if your motif demands more width. Choose whatever shaped edge suits your fancy (animal silhouettes, leaves, flames, waves, abstract geometric shapes, continuous quilt motif, etc.).

3. If the right and left front will be mirror images of the same design, it is only necessary to draw one outside facing. If the right and left are different, draw a facing for each side.

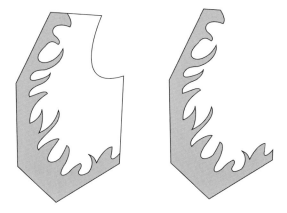

4. Overlay the "drawn on" pattern piece with the pattern tracing material and trace a separate pattern piece for the shaped outside facing.

5. Cut out the garment from fleece.

6. Cut out the shaped outside facings from a contrast fleece. For accuracy, cut a single layer at a time.

a. If the right and left front facings are the same shape mirror-imaged, lay the fleece right side up and the outside facing pattern piece right side up to cut the first facing. Flip over only the facing pattern piece to cut the second facing. Mark the right side of the fabric on both facings.

b. If the right and left front facings are different shapes, cut each facing with the fleece right side up and the facing pattern piece right side up. Mark the right side of the fabric on both facings.

7. At the appropriate point in garment construction, when it is time to sew the facing, hem, or edge finish, place the right side of the outside facing against the wrong side of the garment and pin the raw edges together.

8. Sew with an exact 1/4" seam allowance.

9. Turn the outside facings to the right side of the garment (finished position), rolling the seam slightly towards the wrong side of the garment.

10. Pin the facing in place on the right side of the garment.

11. Topstitch 3/8" from the seamline.

12. Peel back the outside facing and lightly spray KK2000 temporary adhesive spray on the wrong side of the facing. Finger press to adhere it in the finished position. (*Note:* Spray only the wrong side of the facing. Do not spray the fleece garment.)

13. Edgestitch the outside facing in place, stitching close to the blunt edge of the facing.

nancy's note

Your order of construction will vary according to the garment you are sewing. Is the outside facing only on the front, or is it on the back too? Does it go around the back neck edge? Is it at the garment hem or just down the center front? Read through your pattern directions and plan when and where to incorporate the outside facing application.

Fleece Yarn

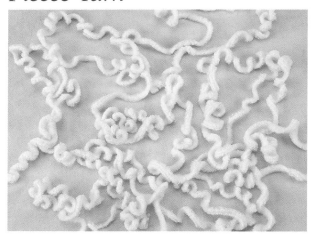

What? Fleece yarn? How? And what do I want it for?

If you cut a narrow strip of fleece on the crossgrain (with the stretch), and then stretch it to the maximum, the fleece strip will curl and gnarl to form a strand of yarn. You can use that yarn for a variety of finishing and embellishment purposes. It

is perfect for delicate edge finishes, button loops, and belt loops. The color match is perfect (it has to be... it's self-fabric!). It also serves as a versatile yarn to couch in place for surface embellishment (see page 76).

Making Fleece Yarn

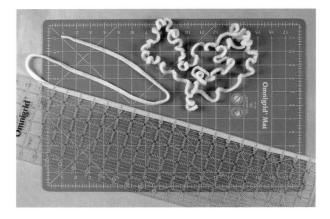

1. Use a rotary cutter to cut exact 3/8" strips of fleece on the crossgrain (from selvage to selvage).

nancy's note

There are not many times when fleece sewing requires precision, but this is one of those times. If you cut skinnier than 3/8", the strip will break when you stretch it hard. If you cut fatter than 3/8", it will be too thick to flow smoothly under a presser foot and too thick for a joining stitch to completely encompass the yarn. Cut an exact 3/8" strip.

2. Grab one end of the fleece strip and pull the strip between pinched fingers, stretching the fleece tightly. The fleece strip will gnarl and curl, forming a strand of yarn.

Fleece Yarn "Crochet" Edge Finish

This is a clever way to mimic the delicate crochet edge finishes found on boiled wool jackets and vests. It is suitable for the center front and bottom edges, armhole edges, sleeve edges, and hood edges.

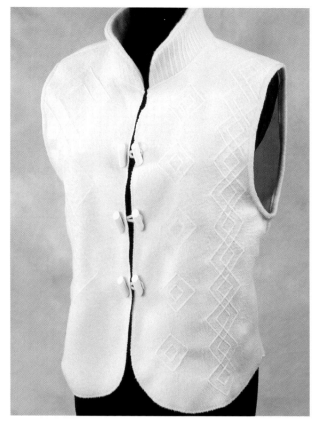

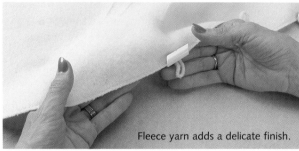

Fleece yarn adds a delicate finish.

Since facings are eliminated, choose a fleece that has enough weight and body to maintain a nice edge as a single layer. This is a lovely, dressier finish for use on indoor vests and sweater jackets.

nancy's note

Experiment on a test sample of fleece before stitching "for real" on your garment. Try various stitches, stitch widths, and stitch lengths until you find one you prefer. Practice stitching around corners and curves, lengthening the stitch as necessary to keep the garment edge laying flat.

1. Cut out the garment as follows (choose those elements that apply to your garment):

a. Eliminate the front facings (cut-on or separate).

b. Eliminate the armhole facings (for vests).

c. Eliminate the bottom hem allowance (cut to the finished length).

d. Eliminate the sleeve hem allowances (cut to the finished length).

e. Eliminate the hood facing (cut-on or separate).

2. When you come to the appropriate point in the garment construction, apply the fleece yarn edge finish to the edge of the garment. With the right side of garment facing up, butt the fleece yarn alongside the raw edge of the garment, and stitch in place as follows:

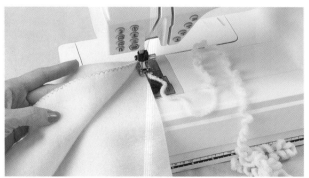

Shown with contrast thread for better visibility.

a. Attach an edgestitch or edge guide presser foot to your machine.

b. Select an open, multiple zigzag stitch to attach the fleece yarn to the garment edge. You want an open, less dense multiple stitch that doesn't distort the fabric edge or stretch the yarn. These types of stitches are generally grouped with the practical and utility stitches on your machines. The stitches may be named jersey, honeycomb, serpentine, universal, elastic, etc.

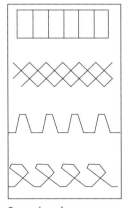

Examples of open stitches.

c. Widen the stitch width to a minimum of 4.0mm. Wider is even better. Experiment as wide as your machine allows. (The stitch swing must be wide enough to completely go over the edge of the fleece yarn and wide enough to come back and take a good bite into the fleece garment.)

d. Lengthen the stitch length to a minimum of 3.0mm. (Your test sewing will indicate the necessary stitch length for a pretty edge finish with no distortion of the fabric edge.)

Other Uses for Fleece Yarn

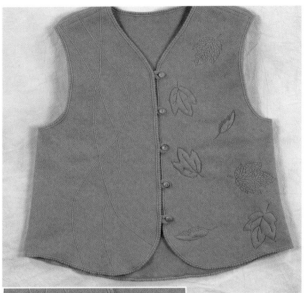

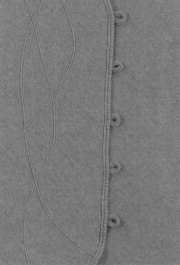

This vest features pintuck embellishment, trapunto motifs, scalloped edge finish, and fleece yarn button loop closures.

Button Loops

Fleece yarn is the perfect choice for button loops. Cut a fleece strip 3/8" wide for a delicate button loop, or 1/2" wide for a sturdier loop. Stretch to form a yarn. Cut into appropriate lengths to slip over your button and stitch loops extending from the garment edge.

You can cut fleece yarn for button loops wider than 3/8" because it will not have to continuously feed underneath a presser foot.

Belt Loops

Fleece yarn makes great belt loops for jackets, robes, etc. Test different widths of fleece until you find one that gives you a finished yarn appropriate for your garment.

Scalloped Edge Finish

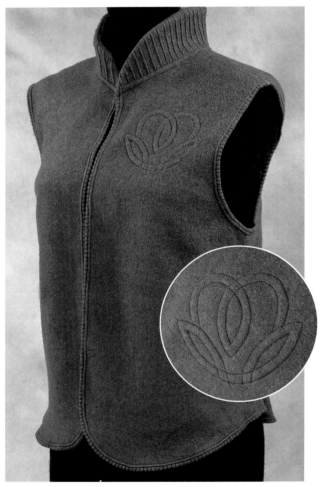

This vest features pintuck collar, trapunto motif, and a scalloped edge finish.

This is a lovely edge finish suitable for center front and bottom edges, armhole edges, sleeve edges, and hood edges.

Eliminate facings and hems as necessary to allow for a 5/8" hem. Choose a fleece that has enough weight and body to maintain a nice edge without facings or hem allowances. This is another lovely finish for use on indoor vests and sweater jackets.

1. When you come to the appropriate point in the garment construction for the edge finish, turn up a 5/8" hem allowance. Working from the wrong side of the fabric, scallop the edge as follows:

a. Set your machine for the blindhem stitch.

b. Set your machine on mirror image. (If you don't have this function on your machine, sew with the bulk of the fabric to the right of the needle rather than the traditional placement to the left of the needle.)

c. Lengthen the stitch length to 4.0mm.

d. Widen the stitch width to 6.0mm. (If your machine can't stitch that wide, adjust as wide as you can.)

e. Moderately increase the needle thread tension.

2. Sewing from the wrong side, stitch so that the straight stitches are on the hem allowance and the swing of the zigzag stitch goes off and completely over the fold of the hem. Sew at a moderate speed (no pedal to-the-metal!), being careful not to stretch the fleece.

3. Insert a 4.0/90 double needle and thread the machine (refer to page 46).

4. To finish with double needle topstitching, sew from the right side of the garment as follows:

a. Choose a straight stitch and adjust to 3.5mm stitch length.

b. Change the tension back to normal setting. (You had increased the tension for the scallop stitching.)

c. With the right toe of the presser foot riding on top of the scallops, and the right needle falling exactly on the straight stitches of the blindhem stitch, double needle topstitch the hem.

d. From the wrong side, trim the excess hem allowance close to the stitching.

Channel Stitched Hems

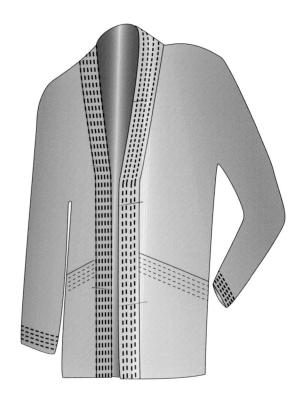

This isn't a new idea – you've used this multiple topstitching finish in many areas of sewing. I've included it in this chapter as a reminder. It's a nice simple finish that adds just a touch of detail and interest to an otherwise plain garment.

When the garment is complete, topstitch multiple rows spaced 3/8" to 1/2" apart. You can stitch three, four, five… or as many rows as you like. Lengthen the stitch length to 4.0mm both for more visibility and to prevent distortion of the fabric. This detail looks lovely on garment hems, sleeve hems, front facings or bands, pocket facings, collars, etc.

Quick Fringe Technique

I featured this super-fast way to fringe fleece in both *Adventures With Polarfleece®* and *More Polarfleece® Adventures*. I am repeating it in *Polar Magic* because you will use it a lot in Chapter 10 – Fleece for the Home.

Materials
* 1 large cutting mat
* 1 smaller cutting mat
* Rotary cutter

1. Lay the fleece on the larger cutting mat.

2. Lay a smaller cutting mat on the fleece, 2", 3", 4" (or whatever depth you want the fringe to be) from the end of the fleece to be fringed.

3. Fold the fleece to be fringed over the smaller mat.

4. Use the rotary cutter to cut the fringe. Cut from the smaller mat and "run" onto the larger mat.

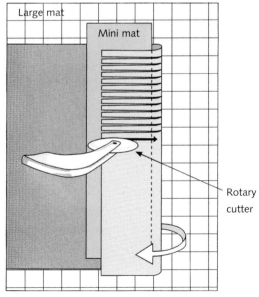

Fold over desired fringe depth

Chapter 7 ❄ Surface Embellishments

An Array of Texturizing Techniques

Sculpturing

When I introduced the idea of sculpturing fleece in *Adventures With Polarfleece®*, everyone was excited about the embellishment opportunities this delightfully easy technique offered. *More Polarfleece® Adventures* greatly expanded the sculpturing idea by incorporating decorative stitches and double needles into the technique. Here, in *Polar Magic*, I return to this favorite technique for more fun.

In the beginning, sculpturing was simply satin stitching on fleece. The stitches sank into the loft of the fleece and created a groove. Those embedded stitches imprinted designs, patterns, and motifs. You were embossing the fleece with stitches.

Sculpturing has expanded into using different functional stitches on your machine as well as free-motion stitching.

Sculpturing Basics

There are only four basic steps to sculpturing. But of course, as creative sewers always do, we'll toss in some alternatives as new ideas come into play. Let's start with the basics, and then expand from there.

1. Cut out the garment sections to be sculpted. Sculpturing is done on cutout garment pieces before construction and on a single layer of fabric. If there is a facing, sculpture the facing separately.

2. Iron Totally Stable (temporary iron-on, tear-away stabilizer) onto the wrong side of the garment piece, behind the areas that are to be sculptured. Use a dry iron, appropriate temperature, and light pressure. Do not touch the iron to the fleece.

3. Satin stitch the design on the right side of the fleece using a 3.0mm to 4mm zigzag width and a shorter stitch length. A hint of fabric should show between the stitches. Loosen the needle thread tension as necessary so the needle thread pulls slightly to the underside.

4. Remove and discard the stabilizer.

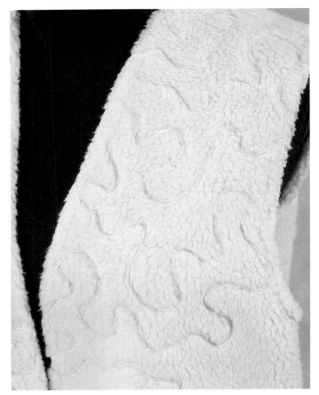
Sculpturing – meandering.

Sculpturing – making grids or plaids.

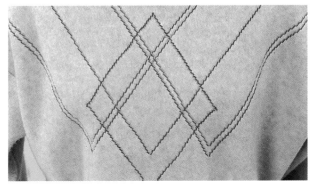
Double needle decorative stitch sculpturing.

Free-motion sculpturing.

In *More Polarfleece® Adventures* I began with simple sculpturing ideas – outlining a print or accenting lines of a plaid. I then made my own "printed fleece" with meandering satin stitching lines resembling stippling but with more definition. I attached a quilt bar to my machine and sculptured grids and plaids. More possibilities became obvious as I started exploring the built-in decorative stitches in my machine. And I saw those possibilities double when I inserted a double needle! And then, on a small scale, I played with free-motion sculpturing.

In this chapter we'll explore even more ways to sculpt and texturize fleece.

❄ "Branding" Fleece

Stitched impressions done on a conventional sewing machine.

Jeanine Twigg, author of *Embroidery Machine Essentials*, discovered a phenomenal fleece texturizing technique when she was playing with an embroidery machine motif. Originally intending to embroider a satin stitch motif, Jeanine stopped after the first series of stitching when she found that the underlay stitches created a wonderful sculptured effect! The fleece looked branded, or stamped.

Underlay stitches are the first group of stitches that lay the groundwork for embroidery machine fill-in satin stitch designs. Their purpose is to sta-

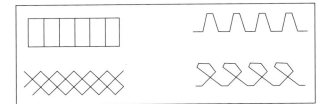

Examples of open stitches.

bilize the design area and maintain the design shape. Underlay stitches are similar to a three-step zigzag or ladder stitch and provide just enough stitches to compress the fleece and create a textured groove.

Since not everyone owns an embroidery machine, I immediately set out to copy this look using a conventional sewing machine.

nancy's hint

Motifs with straight lines are much easier to sew than circular designs. (Does that sound like the voice of experience speaking?)

Choose simplistic, geometric designs to sculpture similar to the templates shown. The goal is to "brand" the fleece with deep grooves created by stitches. However, unlike traditional sculpturing where you fill the groove with noticeable fill-in satin stitching, you are aiming for a subtler look.

Branding Directions

1. To stabilize the fleece, iron Totally Stable to the wrong side of the fleece, behind the design area.

2. Transfer the designs to the fleece using one of the methods from Chapter 3.

3. Choose a decorative thread and appropriate needle.

4. Choose an open, multiple zigzag stitch. These types of stitches are generally grouped with the practical and utility stitches on your machine. They may be named jersey, honeycomb, serpentine, universal, elastic, etc. Widen to at least a 4.0mm stitch width and increase the stitch length. Start with 3.0mm length and test to see what looks good on your fleece.

5. Test "brand" a stabilized fleece sample before sewing for real. Experiment with different stitches to see which ones you prefer.

6. Sew slowly and study the stitch progression. Determine where you want to be "in the stitch" for effectively pivoting corners. (In my test stitching, I eliminated some stitches simply because I could not figure out how to make a good-looking corner!)

7. Adjust the stitch width and length as necessary to achieve a noticeable groove that is easy to sew. If your stitches are uneven and you are using a plastic presser foot, change to a metal foot. I found that metal glides smoothly, whereas plastic sometimes drags a bit.

Branding fleece creates a nice subtle print. You can sprinkle motifs all over a garment, or simply brand collars and cuffs.

Templates for "Branding"

Free-Motion Sculpturing for the F.M.I. (Free-Motion Impaired)

In *More Polarfleece® Adventures* I ventured into the world of dropped feed dogs and free-motion stitching. I placed stabilizer in a small wooden hoop, adhered the fleece, and topped it with Solvy traced with the motif. Pretty soon there were little free-motion trees everywhere!

Marj Ostermiller, a freelance sewing instructor from Billings, Montana, enjoyed teaching the many embellishment techniques shown in her vest. First, she pintucked a few gentle hills, creating a landscape for her free-motion trees. Then, since she had the double needle already in her machine, she pintucked the turn-back portion of the collar, making it look like a wide wale corduroy. Marj serged all the hem edges with a coarse black decorative thread and then turned the hems to the outside of her garment to stitch in place. (It's a great look and her students loved it, too!)

Vest designed by Marj Ostermiller.

Vests designed by Bobbi Kriewald.

Bobbi Kriewald, a freelance sewing instructor in the Seattle area took to heart the motto "There are no mistakes, only design changes." She started out making a vest for her husband, Bryan, by free-motion stitching trees for the background and then machine embroidering a bear from Pfaff Creative Fantasy Card #39 "Wild Animals" and a deer from Pfaff Creative Fantasy Card #21 "Wildlife." All went well until she cut out two backs instead of two fronts! Unable to rescue Bryan's vest, Bobbi decided to make a deer vest for their daughter, Sonja, and a bear vest for their son, Aaron. Bobbi then made another vest for Bryan. Now dad and kids have matching vests! (Bobbi didn't mention if she was up for making a fourth….)

nancy's comment

I have never professed to possess any degree of skill or proficiency when it comes to free-motion stitching. However, I tackled it, and with a little practice and experimentation, had wonderful success, mostly because I concentrated on a small simple motif (bare twiggy winter trees). I had a ball free-motioning winter trees on everything! They were quick. Easy. And, I felt a sense of accomplishment.

I cheated a little on this one. I created a nice landscape on the right side of the vest and decided it needed a little something more. So I pintucked a grid on the left side to showcase four more trees. Here's where I "cheated." I didn't free-motion them. I used the Cactus Punch "Adventures With Fleece" embroidery designs in my embroidery machine and let it do the work for me!

Betty Acheson's pullover with bobbin work.

Betty Acheson, a freelance sewing instructor in the Seattle area, always loves to "push the envelope," putting her own twist on techniques. Betty

is an expert at free-motion stitching and decided to do her embellishment "backwards." Betty's finished stitching is actually bobbin work!

The pattern is called "Upside Down Winterscape" by Cindy Losekamp and is available at Pfaff dealerships. It is a paper pattern that includes complete instructions. Betty traced the design onto Totally Stable and stitch-transferred the motif (see page 26). Except… (here's the great part) she used Candlelight thread in the bobbin! Betty stitch transferred and finished the design all in one step!

Then, one day I saw a gorgeous jacket with a cluster of dramatic tall winter trees on the garment back. I coveted those dramatic trees. However, they were much too big to fit in my little wooden hoop and I was not excited at the prospect of multiple hoopings. I was also sure they required more skill than I had… that is until I found a clever notion called Quilt Sew Easy by Heavenly Notions (see page 20). If you are a free-motion quilter, you already have this in your stash since it was origi-

nally designed for quilting. That's part of the fun of adventuresome sewing – finding crossover uses for techniques and sewing tools.

Stabilizing the fleece twice with Totally Stable gives the firmness necessary to easily move the fleece back and forth. The foam grippers and flexibility of the Quilt Sew Easy provide easy control without hooping the fabric.

This easy tool allowed me to broaden my horizons. Forests instead of single trees. Landscapes. Even backwards bobbin work (like Betty's Winterscape).

Seasoned free-motion embroiderers will be off and stitching while the rest of us are still testing and experimenting. For the novice free-motion stitcher, the simple directions offered below will get you started.

Free-Motion Tall Trees Directions

1. Cut out the fleece garment according to the pattern directions.

2. To stabilize the fleece, iron Totally Stable to the wrong side of fleece, behind the design area.

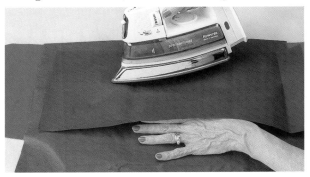

3. For additional stability and easier handling for free-motion stitching, iron a second layer of Totally Stable onto the first layer.

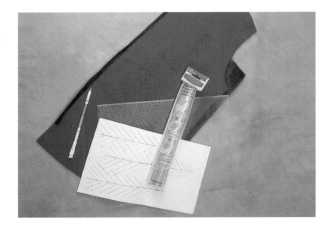

4. Transfer the tall tree designs onto the fleece, using the template provided and one of the methods discussed in Chapter 3. (Transfer mesh and Chacopel pencils work very well.)

5. Thread your machine with a decorative thread and appropriate needle. Loosen the needle tension so that the stitches pull slightly to the underside. Use regular or lightweight bobbin thread in the bobbin.

6. If your machine is in a sewing table, lower it to the flatbed position. If you are sewing on a regular table, attach the sewing machine table or extension plate that came with your machine so you have the largest flat sewing surface possible.

7. Set the machine as follows:

a. Lower the feed dogs.

b. Set the machine for 2.5mm zigzag width. (The stitch length doesn't matter because the feed dogs are lowered and you are in control.)

c. You may attach a darning presser foot, free-motion embroidery presser foot, or choose to stitch using no presser foot at all.

d. Lower the presser foot. (If you are stitching with no presser foot, you must remember to do this to engage the thread tension discs. Since there is no presser foot for reference, it's easy to forget to lower the presser foot that isn't there. The result is a very unpleasant rat's nest on the underside.)

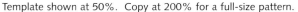

Template shown at 50%. Copy at 200% for a full-size pattern.

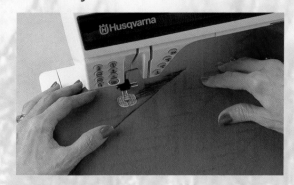

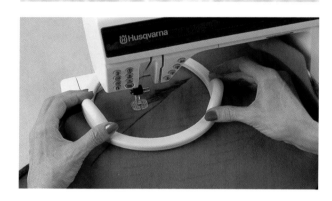

I found my machine offered a free-motion guide foot – a larger plastic presser foot with horizontal and perpendicular grid lines that made it very easy for me to "stay on track" and see where I was stitching.

8. With your elbows resting on the table and hands comfortably holding the handles of the Quilt Sew Easy in the east-west position, center the area to be stitched in the Quilt Sew Easy and begin stitching the tall trees. Move the fabric in a side-to-side motion. Stitch a few rows on the center trunk as a base for stitching the bare branches.

9. Use the main branches as a guideline for the angle of stitching. Fill in as little or as much as you like. Move the Quilt Sew Easy as necessary to stitch the different sections of the trees. Stitch the center trunk again to strengthen its definition.

10. Finish by stitching shadows at the base of the tree, if desired.

11. For a bit more detail, you can add a flock of birds to the sky. You don't have to have an embroidery machine to "embroider" birds. For a great looking bird in flight, choose the satin stitch scallop on your machine. Sew a single scallop for the first wing. Stop with your needle in the fabric. Pivot 90°, or a little less, and sew a second single scallop for the other wing.

12. Remove the tear-away stabilizer from the underside.

13. Finish constructing the garment according to the pattern directions.

nancy's tips

If this is your first experience with free-motion sewing:

* Stay relaxed – you don't need a death grip. It's easy to get stiff and tense. If your teeth hurt, you are taking this too seriously. A glass of chilled white wine, set off to the side (but within reach), helps a lot!

* Free-motion sewing may be uncomfortable at first because you don't have the feed dogs to depend on.

* Sew faster – move slower. Sew at a medium to medium-fast speed and move the Quilt Sew Easy with a slower, smooth, side-to-side motion. The medium to medium-fast speed keeps the stitches from getting too long. The sideways motion keeps the stitches laying neatly on top of each other. Using a grid-marked free-motion presser foot makes it even easier to align the stitches.

* If you don't like the way a stitched line looks, change your angle or movement until you have a look you like. (That's why a test sample is important.)

Embroidery Machine Magic

Clever Ways to Modify Embroidery Machine Designs to Texturize and Sculpt Fleece

As a result of all the excitement surrounding machine embroidery and the popularity of fleece garments, embellishing fleece with embroidery was a natural progression.

In this chapter we'll begin to play with embroidery machine designs, adapting them to texturize and embellish fleece. We aren't doing embroidery the "real" way – we're cheating a little. And the rule is: Know the correct technique before you cheat. Refer to Jeanine Twigg's book, *Embroidery Machine Essentials* for authoritative and comprehensive information on everything you need to know for successful embroidery. It covers the entire embroidery process from choosing designs, threads, stabilizers, and needles, to hooping, design placement, and stitching techniques.

In *More Polarfleece® Adventures*, I devoted an entire chapter to traditional machine embroidery techniques for working with fleece. I discussed fill-in embroidery designs and addressed the challenges of achieving consistent fill stitches on top of lofty napped fabrics. This involved using a variety of toppings to provide a barrier between the fleece and the embroidery stitches.

However, when using embroidery for the purpose of texturizing fleece, the approach changes. Now we are going to contrast the loft of fleece with the compact multiple stitches of embroidery and use this dissimilarity for dimension and texture. For texturizing, choose "spaced" designs with open, unstitched areas that allow the fleece to puff between the stitched areas. Since the desired end result has changed, some of the embroidery techniques will change.

Choosing Embroidery Designs to Add Dimension

To create texture on fleece you need a contrast of depths. This means you need motifs that offer stitched areas alongside unstitched areas. You can find or create this look using many of the embroidery designs you currently have in your embroidery library.

❋ Outline quilt motifs: Use "as is." Since they are simplistic in nature and already designed for the loft of multiple batted layers, they are perfect for fleece texturing.

❋ Appliqué motifs: Use just the underlay stitches of the appliqué motifs or use the underlay stitches, fast forward past the appliqué fabric part, and end with the finishing satin stitches.

❋ Fill-in embroidery motifs: Fast forward through the fill-in stitching and use only the finishing outline stitching.

❋ Lace motifs: Choose simpler designs. Leave uncut those areas that were to be cut away. Fast forward past any bridging stitches that were to enmesh open areas.

❋ Cutwork motifs: Choose simpler designs. Do not cut the "cutout" areas. Fast forward past any support bars that were to be stitched across open areas.

nancy's note

In Chapter 8, on page 93, you will use the same criteria for embroidery designs when doing trapunto on fleece, with the addition of stuffing unstitched areas for even more loft and contrast of depths.

Stabilizer

To add dimension and texture to the fleece, you need a backing that gives permanent stabilization to maintain the depth of the stitches and loft of the areas between the stitching lines.

Choose a *permanent* cut-away stabilizer as opposed to a tear-away or rinse-away stabilizer. A tear-away stabilizer is considered temporary, intended to break down and wash away over time. A permanent backing stabilizes during the stitching process as well as during wearing and laundering. In designs used for texturing, not only do you want to stabilize the area for stitching, but you also want the stabilizer backing to permanently hold the deeply grooved stitches.

Choose a soft stabilizer that doesn't interfere with the character of the fleece and one that allows the embroidered area to remain soft. (You don't need a heavy or stiff stabilizer because you are not piling in a lot of stitches.) When finished, trim away the excess stabilizer close to the outer perimeter of the stitched motif. I prefer Sulky Soft 'n Sheer because it is a textured, nonwoven nylon that is ultra soft next to the skin. It has excellent stretch resistance and eliminates pulling or sagging from the surrounding fabric. (Check the information on your chosen stabilizer to make sure it is a cut-away permanent stabilizer.)

Topping

When doing embroidery on fleece you will not use a topping because you want the stitches to sink into the loft of the fleece. That's what creates the dimension.

In most embroidery situations a topping is used to provide a smooth surface, allowing fill-in embroidery stitches to lie smoothly alongside each other, on top of the nap, and give even coverage. Toppings are films or vinyls that provide a barrier between the fleece and the embroidery stitches. For your purposes here, creating texture, the use of a topping would defeat the goal.

Hoop Size

Choose the smallest hoop possible that accommodates the size of the motif you are embroidering. (Don't be tempted to use a huge hoop thinking that you can sprinkle around a couple small motifs and avoid the multiple hoopings of a smaller hoop. Yes, you will avoid numerous hoopings, but the amount of "play" in the fabric when the hoop dramatically "out sizes" the small motif will adversely affect the quality of the stitches.)

You don't want to hoop the fleece. (It's bulky and cumbersome to hoop, plus you risk the danger of a permanent hoop imprint on the fabric.) So, you will hoop the stabilizer and then use a temporary adhesive spray to adhere the fleece to the stabilizer. (Remember: Always spray adhesive onto the stabilizer, not the fleece.)

Thread Color Choices

Closely matching the thread color to the fleece results in a subtle embossed look. (Be careful on this one. Subtle is classy – hard-to-see is pointless. Choose colors a bit darker than your fleece color.) Contrasting thread colors offer more definition.

For more noticeable stitching in a skeleton (mesh, webbed-look motif) or straight-stitched motif, try one of the following: (Do a test sample to see which works best for your design, thread, and fleece.)

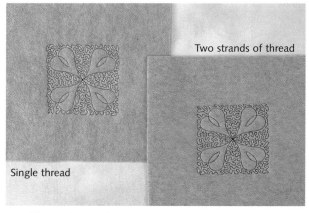

Two strands of thread

Single thread

Motif from Viking Embroidery Disk #101, "Designer Quilt" by Kerstin Widell.

1. Use two strands of thread through the needle. Use a needle one size larger. Do a sample stitching. If you experience thread breakage, try a topstitching needle. (Many factors figure into whether embroidering with two thread strands will be successful – the size of the individual stitches in the design, the intricacy of the design, the weight of the fleece, and the stabilizer. If you have difficulty using two threads, try the next suggestion.)

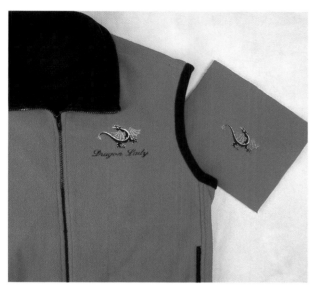

Motif from Viking Embroidery Collection, Ornaments Collection. Test sample: Wings stitched once. Garment: Wings stitched twice.

2. Use a single strand of thread and stitch the webbed area of the motif. Before continuing, stitch the webbed area a second time, resulting in double coverage.

Needle Choice

Choose the needle type according to the type of thread used. Use a 90/14 embroidery, 90/14 metallic, or a topstitching needle for best results.

Fleece Trapunto

Trapunto realistically belongs in this chapter, but there are so many trapunto ideas that it warranted its own chapter. For texturizing using trapunto with conventional sewing machine or embroidery machine, see Chapter 8.

"Adventures With Fleece" Embroidery Design Pack

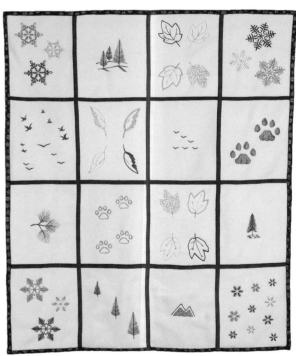

Designs from Cactus Punch, Nancy Cornwell's "Adventures With Fleece" design pack.

I love to "play" with fleece. I enjoy adding classy little touches and subtle embellishments. This is my way of putting my signature on my sewing.

As I was mulling over how to subtly embellish the fleece border prints (featured in Chapter 4.) Lindee Goodall, of Cactus Punch, Inc., suggested I design an embroidery card especially for fleece – motifs that add detail and enhance my border prints, as well as motifs to add a spark to any fleece garment. So that's how Cactus Punch Signature Series #45 – "Adventures With Fleece" embroidery design pack was born.

While I designed these motifs with fleece in mind, they are beautiful on any fabric. Their simplicity and openness of design make them especially suitable for fleece and other lofted fabrics (like quilted cotton, sweatshirting, velour, or velvet). The motifs play up the contrast between the depth of the stitches and the loft of the fabric, creating wonderful dimension.

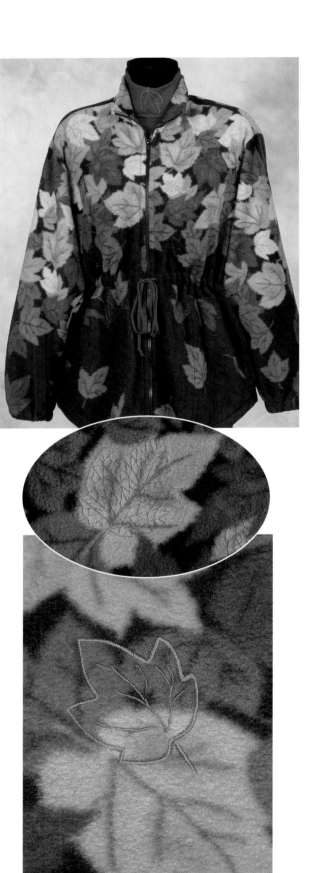

A sprinkling of random snowflakes adds depth and interest.

Embroidered leaves on top of printed ones enhance the feeling of layers of fallen leaves.

Two of my fleece border designs were perfect candidates for mimicking their designs: Autumn Leaves and Snowflakes. The leaf and the snowflake embroidery motifs were taken directly from the fleece prints. They are offered in satin stitch (appliqué), skeleton stitch (mesh), outline stitching (quilting), and fleece texturizing stitch (open multiple compacting stitches like "branding" discussed earlier in this chapter).

When duplicating a print with embroidery motifs, do not attempt to exactly match the motif to the print. It would be virtually impossible! Overlap and offset, but do not try to match. Vary the sizes. Vary the colors.

For an easy way to determine the placement of embroidery motifs, cut out pieces of paper representative of the motif shape and size (snowflake, leaf, paw print, etc.) and scatter the paper pieces around on the garment until you have a balance that appeals to your taste.

Use the Leaves, Snowflakes, or any of the motifs in this series to embellish a solid fleece, creating your own "print."

Choosing matching thread colors results in a subtle tone-on-tone look.

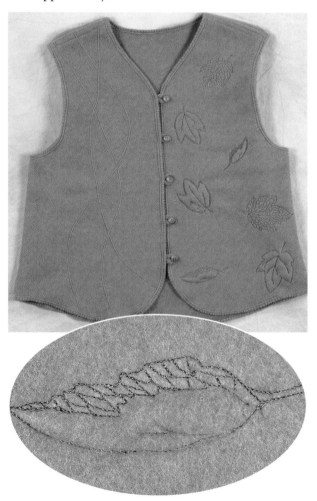

A bit of stuffing in the unstitched areas adds dimension.

Surface Embellishments ❋ 75

Couching With Fleece Yarn

Fleece yarn is a useful "byproduct" of fleece yardage. Fleece yarn can be used to make a lovely crocheted-look edge finish, practical button loops, and belt loops (see page 58). Fleece yarn is also terrific to use as passementerie trim for "dressing up" solid fleeces.

Fleece yarn is made by cutting exact 3/8" strips of fleece on the crossgrain (from selvage to selvage, the direction of most stretch). To make the yarn, pull and stretch the strip hard. It will curl and gnarl to form a strong yarn (refer to page 56).

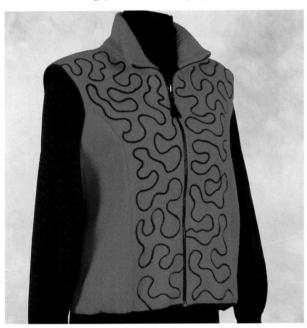

Fleece Yarn Passementerie Trim

A perfect embellishment for collars, pockets, insets, or yokes.

1. Cut out the garment pieces from fleece.

2. From contrast fleece, cut strips of fleece and stretch them to make fleece yarn.

3. Select a presser foot that has a cutout area on the underside to accommodate the bulk of the yarn. (It may be called a braiding foot or cording foot.)

4. Thread the machine with regular thread to match the yarn color, or with clear thread.

5. Beginning at one edge of the garment piece to be embellished, insert one end of the fleece yarn under the presser foot and zigzag in place using a wide and long zigzag stitch. Make sure the swing of the zigzag stitch clears both sides of the yarn. (If the needle bites into the yarn, the yarn becomes chewed and messy looking.)

6. Meander, free-style, avoiding the seam allowance areas until the area is embellished.

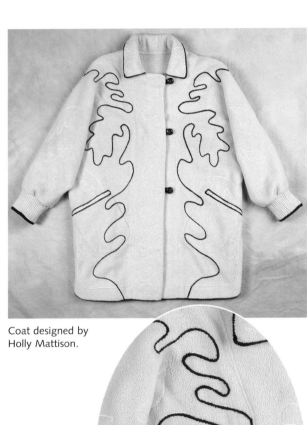

Coat designed by Holly Mattison.

Positive/Negative – Couching/Sculpturing

Holly Mattison began with plain cream fleece and a flowing coat pattern and combined a variety of techniques to create a one-of-a-kind show-stopping garment. (And that is a fact! I saw her in the audience at one of my seminars, stopped what I was doing and asked her to model her wonderful creation. And she was gracious enough to share it in this book.)

Holly credits Barb Fraser and Julie Marett, her instructors at "Pfaff on Granville" in Vancouver, British Columbia, for giving her the inspiration to create her coat. She began with tone-on-tone freeform sculpturing which hinted at leaf shapes. She then used cranberry fleece yarn to couch freeform designs mimicking the sculpturing. To add balance and more drama, she used the yarn to contrast the edges of the coat and the collar. After making polar ribbing cuffs, she wrapped the edges of the cuffs with cranberry fleece to coordinate with the rest of the coat. The matching buttons became an even more dramatic accent when combined with contrast fleece yarn button loops.

Thank you for sharing, Holly. It is gorgeous.

Fleece Chenille

Faux Chenille is a technique developed by Nanette Holmberg using multiple layers of woven rayon or cotton fabrics, stitched together with rows and rows of stitching done on the bias. Then using a rotary cutter or scissors, all but the bottom layer of fabric are slashed open between the stitching lines. When laundered, the multiple layers of slashed fabric ruffle and give a chenille appearance.

You can easily accomplish a chenille effect with fleece. Because fleece is bulky, you only need two layers of fabric. Because fleece does not fray, you can sew and slash in any direction you want. (Woven fabrics are sewn on the bias to inhibit continued fraying.)

Motif from Brother Pacesetter, "Outrageous Outlines." Directions for this pillow are given on page 150.

Because fleece is lofty, it curls up and "blooms" without the need for the laundry to rough-and-tumble it.

Fleece chenille can be used on garments as well as in home dec. The stronger the color contrast between the top layer and the underlayer, the better the end result. Strong color contrast accents the slit openings.

The top fleece layer can be slashed open with sharp scissors, but the cleanest most consistent cuts are made using Omnistrip cutting mats and a rotary cutter. The Omnistrip cutting mats are skinny little strips of cutting mats available in various widths: 1/4", 5/16", 3/8", 1/2", and 5/8".

Sew rows, or channels, of stitching 1/8" wider than the Omnistrip you are going to insert. Sew 1/2" rows for the 3/8" strip. Sew a generous 3/8" for 5/16" strips, etc. After sewing the rows, insert an Omnistrip mini cutting strip between the fleece layers. Using a rotary cutter, carefully cut down the center of each row. The Omnistrip protects the underlayer of fleece from being cut.

I experimented sewing the rows in various widths, as well as on the straight-of-grain, cross-grain, and 45° bias. I found:
❋ Bias lines are the prettiest.
❋ Bias slits seem to allow more light in to show the under color. Since raveling is not an issue with fleece, all the grain lines work. However those rows cut and slashed on the bias were a bit more visible, whereas the straight and cross grains tended to lie closed.

❋ Straight lines give a more consistent look than curved lines. If curved lines are part of your motif, the slashing must be done with scissors.

❋ Narrower is prettier. All widths of rows worked, but the generous 3/8" channels combined with the 5/16" gave the nicest result. I found the 1/4" mat difficult to cut on due to the bulk of fleece. The widest strips resulted in a chunky look.

Directions for Fleece Chenille Designs

1. You need two layers of fleece in contrasting colors. The size of the underlayer must be 2" larger than the motif and can be placed behind the fleece (contrasting color to peek through the main garment color as seen in the Zebra Pillow and Tree Pullover) or on top of the main garment piece (with the main color peeking through the slashes as seen in the Mountain Scene Pullover).

2. Trace a simple design or shape onto the right side of the top layer of fleece using your favorite transfer method from Chapter 3. (The garment sizing will not be affected so there is no need to chenille first and cut out second.)

3. Sew parallel rows of straight stitching to fill the design area. Space the rows approximately 1/8" wider than the Omnistrip you intend to use.

4. Use appliqué or embroidery scissors to neatly trim the excess contrast fleece close to the outermost stitching lines.

5. Slip an Omnistrip cutting mat between the fleece layers. This can be done in a variety of ways, depending upon your design.

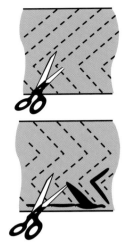

a. If your motif offers an entrance place (the cut edge of the garment, or at the end of the design), insert the cutting strip there.

b. If your design is completely "enclosed" with no entrance place, carefully make an entrance place by starting a cut with the small point of scissors. Be careful to cut only the top layer.

c. If your design has angle changes (corners, zigzags), insert the cutting strip and cut until the channel changes directions. Using the small point of scissors, make a small clip at the new angle and reinsert the cutting strip to cut the new channel.

It's as easy as that! Texture with a little surprise of contrast color peeking through!

Chenille Projects

Snowflake motifs from Cactus Punch, Nancy Cornwell's "Adventures With Fleece" design pack.

These chenille projects offer a variety of looks and approaches to doing the technique. When beginning a design of your own, read through all the projects and choose a method that fits your circumstances.

Chenille Tree

Contrast fleece is placed behind the garment main fabric. The motif is then stitched with rows of channel stitching. The fabric between the stitching lines is slashed open to reveal the contrast color peeking through.

Additional Materials
❋ Piece of contrast fleece at least 2" larger than the tree motif

Directions
1. Cut out the garment pieces from fleece.

2. Transfer the tree motif on page 80 to the garment, centering it on the garment front. Check the pattern directions to see if the neckline will be trimmed during construction. Place the top of the tree 3" to 5" below where neckline seam will be.

3. Cut a piece of contrast fleece at least 2" larger than the finished tree size. (No need to be exact since the excess will be trimmed away.)

4. Place the contrast fleece behind the design area, with the right side of the contrast fleece against the wrong side of the garment fleece. Pin to secure.

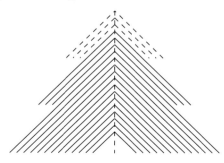

5. Stitch the top three rows (resulting in two sewn channels), pivoting at the top. Backtack at the beginning and end of stitching. Stitch rows a generous 3/8" apart. Make sure the rows start and end at the same level.

6. Stitch the next three rows as in Step #5.

nancy's note
If it seems that your pivot point is straying off center front, don't worry. A slight difference will never be noticeable. It is more important to keep the channel rows consistent.

7. Stitch the third set of channel rows, continuing to sew rows until the legs of the inverted "V" (center bottom of tree) are about 1-1/2" to 2" apart.

8. Draw stitching lines for the tree trunk and stitch.

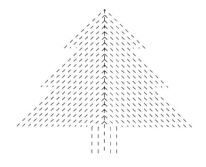

9. From the wrong side of garment, trim the excess contrast fleece close to the stitching.

10. On the right side of the fabric, make a small starting cut at the beginning of each channel using sharp scissors. Insert a 5/16" Omnistrip and care-

nancy's note
Alternative method: In this particular motif you could insert the Omnistrips into the channels from the wrong side of the garment, and then turn the garment right side up to slash the channels open. Just pay attention to what you are doing. The procedure seems obvious, but it is easy to fall into a rhythm, and suddenly insert a cutting strip and just slash without first turning the garment over to cut on the right side! (Hmm... Does this sound like the voice of experience talking?)

Chenille Tree
1/2 template

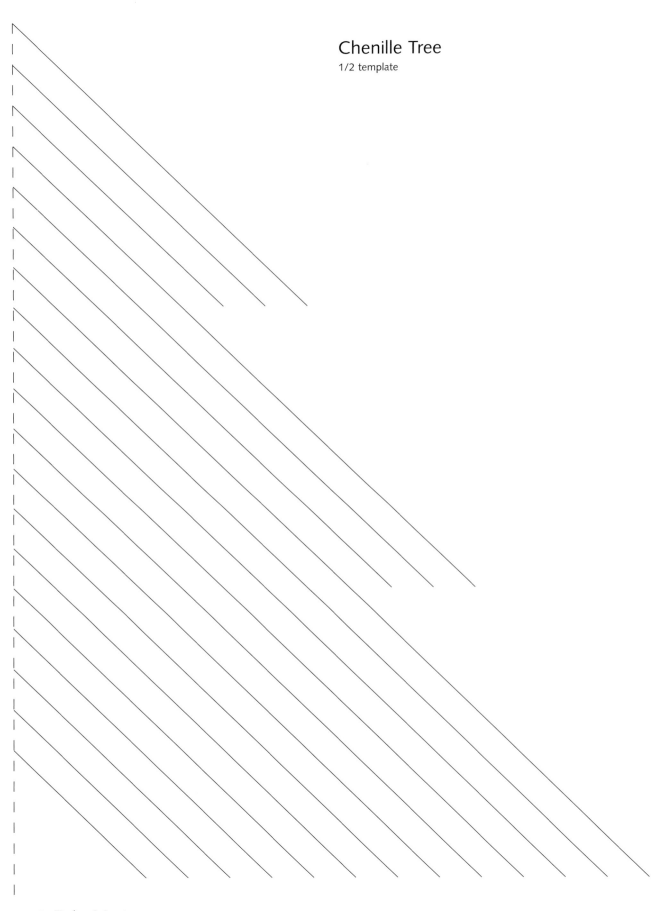

fully slash open the top layer of fleece with a rotary cutter. Use scissors to cut open the tree trunk.

11. Finish the garment per the pattern instructions.

Tree Variation

The contrast fleece for the tree could have been placed on the right side of the garment, as was done on the following Mountain Scene.

Chenille Mountain Scene Appliqué

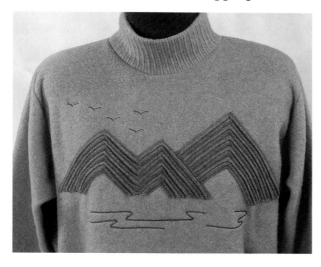

The stitching on this garment is pretty much the same as the Chenille Tree, except that the contrast fleece is placed on the right side of the garment (like an appliqué) rather than on the wrong side. The motif is then stitched with rows of channel stitching and trimmed around the edges. The fabric between the stitching lines is then slashed open to reveal the garment color peeking through the contrast chenille appliqué. Satin stitch lines sculpture the lake.

Additional Materials
❋ Piece of contrast fleece 2" larger than the mountain range
❋ Totally Stable stabilizer, 1/2 yard
❋ Rayon thread to match contrast fleece color
❋ 90/14 embroidery needle

Directions
1. Cut out the garment pieces from fleece.

2. Transfer the mountain range on page 83 onto

the right side of the contrast fleece. *Note:* The contrast fleece is larger than the mountain scene motif. It will be trimmed to size after stitching.

3. Place the traced mountain piece onto the garment front, mountain fleece right side up and garment fleece right side up.

4. Sew rows of stitching a generous 3/8" apart, pivoting at the mountain tops and backtacking at the beginning and end.

5. Using appliqué or embroidery scissors, trim the contrast fleece close to the outer stitching lines.

nancy's note

In other scenarios, I would have sculpture stitched the lake first and then sewn the mountain range. However, in practice, I have found that as I stitch chenille rows, I sometimes take creative license and extend a bit further than drawn, or change an angle, or add (or subtract) a line or two. I like the freedom to alter the design as I am sewing. Tracing and sculpturing the lake as the last step allows me to change the placement or size to compensate for any creative license I may have taken with the mountains.

6. Insert 5/16" cutting strips and slash open the channels.

7. Transfer the lake motif below the mountain range.

8. Press Totally Stable (temporary iron-on, tear-away stabilizer) on the wrong side of the fleece, behind the lake area.

9. With regular thread in the bobbin and decorative thread to match the contrast mountain color, satin stitch the lake. Use a zigzag stitch 3.0mm to 4.0mm wide and a less dense satin stitch.

10. Satin stitch abstract birds in the sky (refer to page 70).

11. Remove and discard the Totally Stable.

12. Finish the garment, following the pattern directions.

Stained Glass Imagery

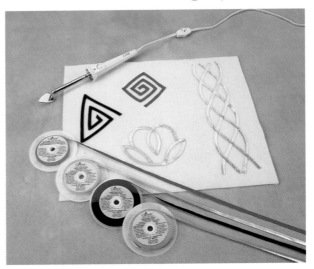

Many of the designs and motifs featured in this book can be used in multiple ways. Trapunto, sculpturing, pintucking for texture. Stained Glass Imagery offers yet another type of embellishment.

Take the branding motifs from page 65, the Celtic Tulip motif from page 90, or the Sunflower motif from page 143, and turn it into an elegant "leaded glass" design.

The directions that come with the Mini Iron, Quick Bias trim, and Appliqué Sheet (pages 20-21) tell you everything you need to know. All you need to do is choose which design you want to do first.

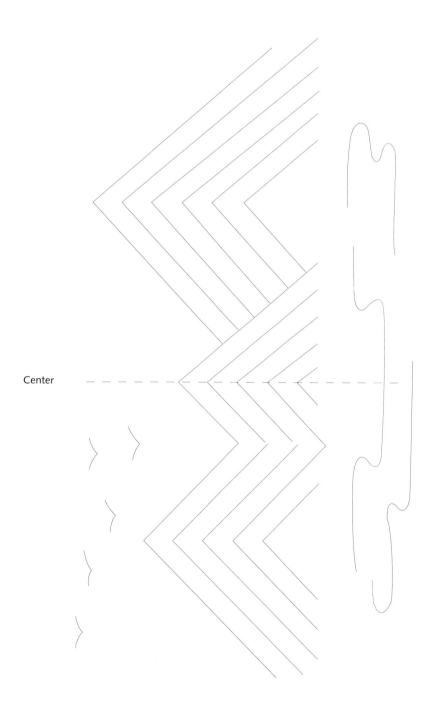

Center

Template shown at 50%. Copy at 200% for a full-size pattern.

Chapter 8

TRAPUNTO

Motif from Viking Embroidery Disk #112, "Lace Designs" by Jeanne Harrison.

Motifs from Viking Embroidery Disk #101, "Designer Quilt" by Kerstin Widell.

Motif from Viking Embroidery Disk #101, "Designer Quilt" by Kerstin Widell.

*F*leece is such a forgiving fabric that it allows you to achieve a variety of surface effects that add interest and personality to otherwise plain fabric. You can add texture and depth by applying techniques traditionally reserved for other fabrications and using them on fleece. Trapunto is a fun texturizing technique that takes on a new personality when used on fleece. Traditionally speaking, trapunto is a type of quilting where a simple design is outline stitched. Stuffing is then inserted from the backside, plumping the unstitched areas and giving high relief. The result is a lovely raised motif. Trapunto is perfect for those times when you want to add a little something extra but still want to be subtle.

Fleece is a great "canvas" to explore this art form. There is a tremendous variety of approaches you can take, using an assortment of sewing notions, machines, and techniques. And you can use either a conventional sewing machine or embroidery machine.

For trapunto, you need two layers of fabric – the fleece face plus a stable backing to provide a "pocket" for the stuffing. You'll stitch motifs that offer open unstitched areas that you can lightly stuff or pad to give depth and dimension to the motif.

Choosing the Motif

When choosing a motif for trapunto, choose a simpler design that lends itself to creating dimension. Select designs that offer medium to large unstitched areas that you can stuff. Narrower tunnel-like channels can be filled with a single or double strand of yarn. Larger areas can be filled with back-and-forth rows of yarn or stuffed with batting.

Avoid lots of tiny open areas. Besides being difficult to insert stuffing into, they cannot offer contrast of height and depth. Simpler is better and more effective.

Good Design Choices

* Quilting designs
* Simple Celtic designs
* Simple flowers with multiple petals
* Embroidery machine quilting motifs

Choosing the Fleece

Choose a mid-weight to lightweight solid color fleece with a flat rather than textured surface. Heavy fleece becomes too bulky with the addition of stuffing.

Trapunto shows best on light to mid-toned colors. The light refraction shows the depths well. If choosing a darker color fleece, test on a sample first to make sure contrasting depths will be visible and which color thread looks best.

Choosing the Thread

The stitching lines sink into the loft of the fleece, resulting in a very subtle grooved effect. Using regular thread a bit darker than the fleece is the most subtle. For a hint of contrast, use a dark thread in the same color family as the fleece. Rayon thread, being heavier than regular thread, is a bit more noticeable.

For the most noticeable stitching lines, use two spools of a darker color rayon thread. Thread as you would for a double needle, but go through the single eye of the needle.

nancy's note

The rule is: When using two strands of thread, go up one needle size. Since you are already using a larger 90/14 needle for fleece sewing, it is not necessary to "size up" again. However, if you find the thread shreds or breaks when stitching, and there are no burrs on your needle or rough spots on your stitch plate, change to a larger size needle.

Choosing the Stabilizer

Choose a soft permanent cut-away stabilizer that does not interfere with the hand of the fleece. You need a cut-away stabilizer because the stabilizer remains an integral part of our design. It will act as both a stabilizer for the stitching and serve as a backing to create a pocket to house the stuffing. (Tear-away stabilizers are considered temporary and break down over multiple launderings.)

I prefer Sulky Soft 'n Sheer because it is a textured, nonwoven nylon that is ultra soft next to the skin. It has excellent stretch resistance and eliminates pulling or sagging from the surrounding fabric not only during the stitching process, but also during the washings and wearings. (Check the information on your chosen stabilizer to make sure it is a cut-away permanent stabilizer.)

Motif Placement

Center a medium to larger motif on a plain front garment, 2" to 3" below the neck seamline. Place a small motif on the left upper front, at the chest pocket area. Center a motif on a pocket. Place a small motif on a collar.

nancy's note

Since you will be applying the trapunto design to the flat garment front before construction, refer to your pattern directions to see if the neckline will be trimmed before adding ribbing or a facing. If so, use a fabric marker to draw in the finished seamline on the wrong side of your garment as a reference point for motif placement.

Motif from Elna EnVision Card #106, "Quilting."

Stuffing Material Choices

There is more than one right stuffing choice. Use what makes sense and seems the easiest to use in each situation. Depending upon the size of the unstitched area you have to fill, and how "raised" you want that area to be, you can use strands of yarn, bits of stuffing, or pieces of batting to puff the unstitched area.

Yarn is great for stuffing hard-to-stuff areas. The needle is easy to maneuver in and out of smaller places.

nancy's note

I choose white yarn since white works well with every color fleece, with no worry about color show through. Using a dark color yarn behind a lighter color fleece risks unwanted shadowing.

Filling Small to Medium Areas

1. Thread a tapestry needle with 4-ply acrylic yarn. Choose a needle with a large enough eye to accommodate the yarn.

2. Using one or two strands of yarn (depending on the width of the channels and how much you want to plump the area), from the wrong side of the garment insert the needle into the Soft 'n Sheer backing, between the stitching lines. Slide the needle through the entire section where filling is desired. The needle and filling yarn are between the stabilizer and the garment fabric. Be careful not to pierce the garment fabric.

3. Pull the yarn into place, filling the entire section and leaving a short yarn tail at the entry hole.

4. Cut the yarn at the entrance and exit holes, leaving 1/4" yarn tails.

5. Gently tug the fleece so the yarn tails disappear into the filled section. If necessary, push the yarn tails in, using the blunt end of the needle.

6. If you need to fill a longer area, continue the next "fill" by going into the exit hole you just came out of. Continue the segments until the entire area is filled.

7. In areas that taper to narrow points (leaves, petals, etc.), enter with the yarn at the wider area of the design and exit at the point.

Use the Filling Narrow Channels directions, except "snake" the yarn back and forth, keeping the rows close to each other, until the entire area is filled.

Filling Medium to Large Areas With Stuffing

Motifs from Viking Embroidery Disk #101, "Designer Quilt" by Kerstin Widell.

Use stuffing to lightly fill medium to larger unstitched areas of a design. In medium to larger areas, stuffing is easier than snaking yarn back-and-forth, and offers the opportunity for a smoother fill. Choose a high quality polyester stuffing. Avoid pellet-type, lumpy stuffing, as it will give the fleece surface a bumpy appearance.

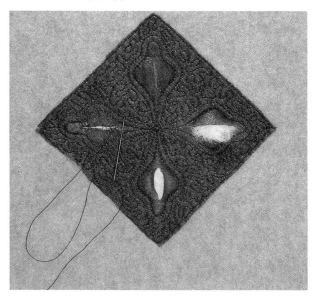

1. Being very careful to cut only the stabilizer, cut a slit in the center of the area to be stuffed.

2. Gently insert the stuffing, filling the unstitched area as plump as desired.

3. Hand stitch the slit closed.

Trapunto With Batting

Motif from Brother Pacesetter Card #29, "Lace Designs."

Batting offers a great "cheater's way" to get the trapunto look without having to insert yarn or stuffing. It is perfect for motifs with larger unstitched design areas or with numerous areas to stuff. Choose high quality soft poly, cotton/poly, or cotton batting with a low to medium loft. Avoid high loft batting, as it is a bulky when combined with fleece.

1. Lightly spray Soft 'n Sheer permanent cut-away stabilizer with KK2000 temporary adhesive and adhere a layer of batting.

2. Lightly spray the batting with KK2000 and adhere the wrong side of the fleece to the batting.

3. Stitch the motif.

4. Trim the excess batting and stabilizer.

nancy's comment

Don't tangle yourself up thinking there is only "one right way" to do things. Many of the best creations happen at midnight when the house is quiet and you must make do with what is in your stash. If you don't have stuffing, use multiple strands of yarn or shred some batting. If you don't have batting, use another layer of fleece and pretend it's batting. If it makes sense, try it. Who knows, after experimenting a little, you may come up with new techniques and find yourself writing the next book!

Traditional Trapunto With a Conventional Sewing Machine

This vest features trapunto, scalloped edge finish, and a pin-tucked collar.

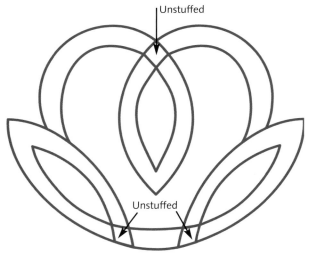

Copy at 165% for a full-size pattern

The Celtic Tulip is shown many ways on page 92. The stitching directions are the same. The difference is in the choice of stuffing. The subtle motif features yarn-filled narrow channels, while the bolder motif features stuffing in the larger areas for more depth contrast.

nancy's note

Trapunto embellishment is done on a cutout garment piece (front, pocket, collar, etc.), before construction. Since it does not affect the width or length of the fabric piece, you can cut out first and trapunto second. Although it is awkward to work on a finished garment, trapunto embellishment could be applied after the fact.

1. Cut a piece of Soft 'n Sheer at least 2" larger than the motif on all sides.

2. Transfer the motif onto the fleece or stabilizer according to the desired end result:

a. Regular thread – If stitching the motif with a single strand of regular thread, trace the motif on the stabilizer and stitch from the wrong side of the garment.

b. Decorative thread – If stitching the motif with one or two strands of decorative thread, transfer the design onto the right side of the fleece and stitch the motif from the right side of the garment.

3. Adhere Soft 'n Sheer to the wrong side of the fleece in the designated motif area.

4. Sew the motif with a shorter straight stitch (2mm to 2.5mm stitch length). Sew all the marked lines, outline stitching the design. Do not backtack. Pull the thread tails to the backside and tie off.

5. Trim the stabilizer backing to 1/4" around the entire outer edge of the design. (Leave the inner portions intact.)

6. Stuff the chosen areas with yarn or stuffing.

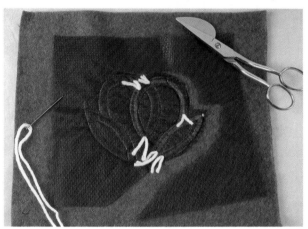

Hints for Successful Narrow Channel Motifs

To create a successful motif with narrow channels for trapunto (double rows of stitching with yarn plumping the area between):

1. Choose a simple motif. Quilting or Celtic designs are great places to start. Take into consideration how many "crossover sections" there are. Every time your stitching line crosses another stitching line, it involves a start and stop when you are filling with yarn. It's not difficult to fill, just tedious. If your design has a lot of crossovers that create small segments, you will lessen the raised effect of the inserted yarn.

2. Draw motif lines 1/4" to 3/8" apart from each other. (This is a nice separation between stitching lines. It is narrow in appearance yet gives enough space to plump with yarn.)

3. For easy and consistent spacing between the stitching lines: After sewing the first stitching line, align the outer right edge of your presser foot alongside the first stitching line. Change the needle position until the needle is directly over the second drawn stitching line. When sewing, guide the presser foot along the first stitching line rather than watching the needle try to pierce the drawn line.

"Cheater's" Trapunto With a Conventional Sewing Machine

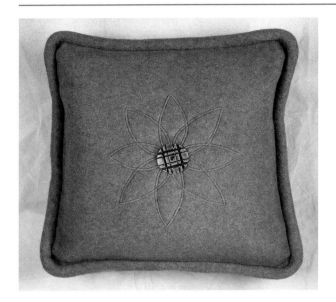

This is called "cheater's" because instead of stuffing an area, you put batting behind the entire design area, stitch the motif, then trim away in those areas you don't want raised. Choose motifs with medium to larger unstitched design areas. Avoid designs that have intricate areas to trim the batting away.

1. Cut a piece of Soft 'n Sheer stabilizer at least 3" larger than the motif on all sides.

2. Transfer the motif onto fleece or stabilizer according to the desired end result:

a. Regular thread – If stitching the motif with a single strand of regular thread, trace the motif on the stabilizer and stitch from the wrong side of the garment.

b. Decorative thread – If stitching the motif with one or two strands of decorative thread, transfer the design onto the right side of the fleece and stitch the motif from the right side of the garment.

3. Cut a piece of batting the same size as the Soft 'n Sheer in Step #1.

4. Lightly spray Soft 'n Sheer with KK2000 temporary adhesive and adhere the batting.

5. Lightly spray the batting with KK2000 and adhere the wrong side of the fleece to the batting.

6. Sew the motif with a shorter straight stitch (2mm to 2.5mm stitch length). Do not backtack. Pull the thread tails to the backside and tie off.

7. Trim the excess stabilizer and batting to 1/4" around the entire outer edge of the design and from the areas you don't want raised.

nancy's note

The Celtic Tulip on page 90 presents the basic technique of trapunto using a conventional sewing machine. The fun starts when you play and vary the embellishment technique to see what happens. Alter the technique to fit the design and appearance you are looking for.

1. Trapunto - Filled narrow channels, page 92.

2. Trapunto - Inner areas plumped with stuffing, page 88.

3. Satin Stitch Sculpturing, page 62.

4. Pintucking for Texture - More Polarfleece® Adventures, page 55.

5. Stained Glass Imagery, page 82.

Trapunto With an Embroidery Machine

There are many embroidery designs that can be used to create lovely trapunto effects on fleece.

Embroidery quilting motifs are obvious choices since they are already designed to contrast the loft of the batting with the depth of the stitching. However, don't limit yourself to only these designs.

Don't restrict yourself to design usage according to what is designated on the packaging by an embroidery or machine company. Have fun by looking beyond the obvious. Study motifs that were designed for an entirely different purpose and see how you can modify them for trapunto.

As I said in Chapter 7, Surface Embellishments, you aren't doing embroidery the "real" way – you're cheating a little. And the rule is: Know the correct technique before you cheat. Refer to the book *Embroidery Machine Essentials* by industry embroidery expert Jeanine Twigg, for authoritative and comprehensive information on everything you need to know for successful embroidery. The book covers the entire embroidery process, from choosing designs, threads, stabilizers, and needles, to hooping, design placement, and stitching technique. And then… cheat a little.

Embroidery Machine Motif Choices

To be effective for trapunto, the design should offer open unstitched areas to stuff for added loft. Oftentimes, by simply skipping past some of the embroidery steps, you can get exactly what you need.

Fill-in embroidery motifs: Designs that offer larger areas of fill stitches are easy to adapt for use with trapunto. Stitch the outline of the motif and fast forward past the fill stitches. Insert a little bit of stuffing. Stitch the inner detail, if applicable. If you experience skipped stitches or broken needles, either remove some of the stuffing or increase the size of your needle. Finish with the outer satin stitching or outline stitching.

Motif from Cactus Punch, Animals design #2002C Horse.

Quilting motifs: These are perfect designs with lots of opportunity to play. Since quilting motifs presume there is loft from batting, the designs are geared to accent the contrast between the sinking of the stitches and the loft of the batting. If you embroider quilt motifs on fleece, you will automatically have a subtle contrast of heights. For the greater depth of trapunto, back the fleece with Soft 'n Sheer, then lightly stuff the open unstitched areas.

Designs from Viking Embroidery Disk #101, "Designer Quilt" by Kerstin Widell.

Quilting motifs with stippling: Some embroidery quilt motifs incorporate stippling into their design, offering even more drama and contrast to the stuffed areas. If you love a quilt motif that doesn't offer stippled areas, add them yourself! Either free-motion stipple or choose the stippling stitch on your machine.

Designs from Viking Embroidery Disk #101, "Designer Quilt" by Kerstin Widell.

Appliqué motifs: Because appliqué motifs tend to be on the simple side, they are perfect for trapunto. Back with Soft 'n Sheer, then outline stitch. Eliminate the overlay appliqué fabric step. Lightly stuff. Finish with the inner detail stitching, if applicable. Depending on the sequence of stitching, you can insert the stuffing before or after the outer satin stitching is sewn.

Motif from Cactus Punch, Mary Mulari's "Nature Appliqué."

Cutwork motifs: Choose simpler cutwork designs with larger designated "cutout" areas, but instead of cutting out the cutout areas, stuff them! Fast forward past any support bars that were to be stitched across the open areas.

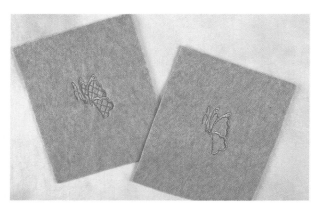

Design from Cactus Punch, Cutwork design #1006 Butterfly.

Lace motifs: Choose simpler rather than intricate lace motifs. Leave uncut those areas that were to be cut open and filled with bridging stitches. Instead, lightly stuff and fast forward past the bridging stitches. You can find many lovely "lace" leaves and flowers that work well for trapunto.

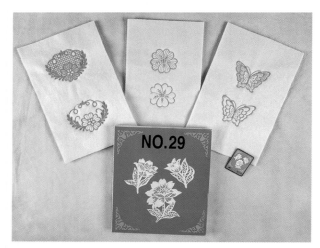

Designs from Brother Pacesetter Card #29, "Lace Designs."

Block letter motifs, banners, and crests: Whether they were intended as appliqué or fill-in embroidery, use only the outer satin stitching and stuff to give loft to the center areas.

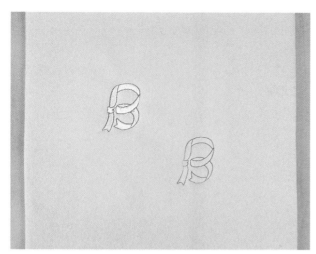

Design from Cactus Punch, "Monogram Essentials - Heirloom."

General Directions for Embroidery Machine Trapunto

To keep the surface taut and secure for general machine embroidery, it is necessary to hoop the fabric. However, when it comes to embroidery on fleece, you must change the hooping process. Since fleece is bulky to hoop, and because the hoop ring might crush the nap and leave an unwanted hoop imprint, you are going to *hoop the stabilizer rather than the fleece*.

1. Tautly hoop Soft 'n Sheer stabilizer.

2. Lightly spray KK2000 temporary adhesive onto the stabilizer and adhere the wrong side of the fleece, making sure the motif is centered in the hoop.

3. Attach the hoop to the embroidery machine.

4. For added stability, machine baste the perimeter of the design (if your machine offers this feature).

5. Stitch the motif.

6. Trim the stabilizer to 1/4" around the outer edges of the design and stuff using one of the methods discussed on page 88.

Trapunto Gallery: A Collection of Trapunto Styles & Techniques

Presented here are a variety of trapunto designs, techniques, and effects. Included are helps, guidelines, and directions to use these ideas as a springboard for adapting other motifs.

Argyle Trapunto Pullover

Take butter-soft heather fleece, add the excitement of embroidery, mix in the flavor of quilting, toss in a pinch of texture, add a hint of classic argyle, and you have the ingredients for a fun garment with a fresh new look.

For more visible stitching lines, I used two strands of a darker colored 40-weight rayon thread with a 90/14 embroidery needle.

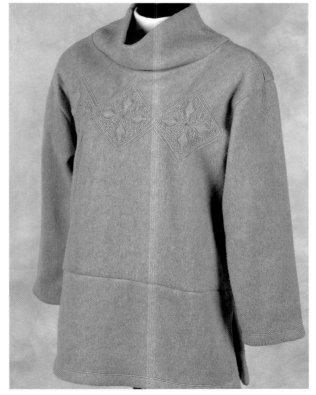

Motif from Viking Embroidery Disk #101, "Designer Quilt" by Kerstin Widell.

This 4" square quilt motif was the perfect size to turn on its side, transforming it into a diamond motif. Then I "tripled it" to get an argyle flavor. Since the stippling was built into the design, all I had to do was lightly stuff the open areas for dimension. The "framework" was made with two rows of 4.0 double needle topstitching.

The general rule is to use the smallest hoop possible for the design you are embroidering. The motif I chose here indicated using a smaller hoop, but because the motifs were arranged on an angle and in a progression, using a larger hoop allowed me more freedom to move the motif as necessary for alignment.

If you choose a design that can be rotated 45°, simply adhere your garment to the hooped stabilizer, placing the garment straight-of-grain up and down in the hoop and rotate the square to change it to a diamond.

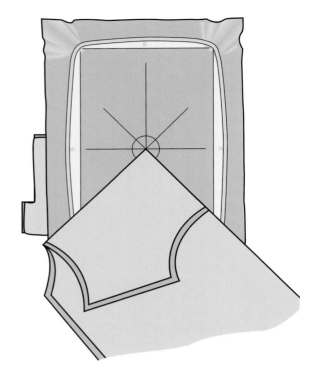

"Lace" Trapunto

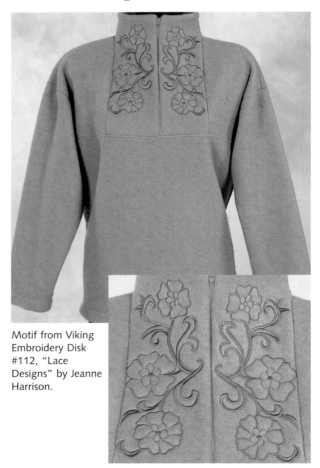

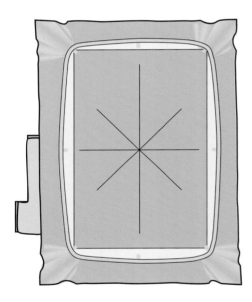

If your chosen design doesn't rotate, place the hooped stabilizer on a gridded cutting mat, align the hoop arrows or notches with the mat grid lines (they show through the stabilizer), and trace horizontal, vertical, and diagonal lines.

Adhere your garment "on the bias" to turn the square motif and make it into a diamond motif.

Motif from Viking Embroidery Disk #112, "Lace Designs" by Jeanne Harrison.

This garment offered a front yoke that presented a wonderful canvas for embellishment. I was looking for something a bit dramatic and easily adapted this large, strong lace motif.

When I compared the overall dimension of the lace motifs to the size of the yokes, it was a pretty tight fit. Rather than court disaster, instead of cutting out the fleece yokes first and embroidering second, I embroidered on a piece of fleece first and cut out the yokes second.

1. Using a fabric marker, lightly trace the yoke outline on the fleece.

2. Plan the placement of the motif and draw intersecting horizontal and vertical lines on the traced yoke to designate the center of the motif.

3. Hoop Soft 'n Sheer stabilizer. Draw in the center mark on the hooped stabilizer. Spray with adhesive and adhere the traced fleece, matching the center marks.

4. If your machine offers a perimeter check or baste feature, double check the design placement.

5. On this particular motif the machine first satin stitches all the leaves and vines then outline stitches the upper flower and comes to a programmed stop. (The machine assumes it is being used as a lace design.)

6. Remove the hoop from the machine and lightly stuffed outer petals.

7. Replace the hoop and satin stitch the outer petals. Do not unhoop the fabric.

8. Watch the stitch progression closely. Stop when the outer petals are finished satin stitching. Fast forward (skipping the inner petal fill-in stitching), and stitch only the center fill-in dot.

9. Repeat the flower procedure for the remaining two flowers.

10. Repeat the above steps to embroider the second traced fleece yoke, mirror imaging the design.

11. Cut out the trapunto embroidered fleece yokes. (Easy cutting hint: Cut out one fleece yoke and use it as the pattern to cut the second yoke. Place the fabric right sides together, exactly matching the embroidery motifs.)

nancy's lesson learned

I concentrated so much on mirror-imaging and matching my leaves and flowers, making sure that the motifs fit into the yoke, that it wasn't until I was completely finished that I noticed I hadn't inserted the zipper evenly on both sides! So my motifs aren't the exact same distance away from the zipper. It's okay... but not perfect. Next time I'll pay as much attention to the garment construction as I did to the embroidery!

Falling Leaves Go-With-Everything Vest

Designs from Cactus Punch, Nancy Cornwell's "Adventures With Fleece" design pack.

You can never have too many denim-friendly vests. And this vest takes advantage of many techniques covered in this book.

The embroidery on this vest was taken from Cactus Punch Signature Series card #45 "Adventures With Fleece" that I designed specifically with fleece in mind. The leaves were embroi-

dered with a twist/tweed rayon thread, employing a wide variety of trapunto techniques. Some leaves used the appliqué method (without the appliqué fabric), some were outline stitched with batting backing. The skeleton leaves (mesh look) simply "embossed" the fleece with their stitches. The end result was an autumn assortment of leaf shapes and effects tumbling down the left side of the vest.

The right side of the vest is graced with freeform pintucks waving down the shoulder (4.0/90 double needle, 3.5mm stitch length, sewing with the nap). The scalloped edge finish technique can be found on page 58. The fleece yarn button loops directions can be found on page 56.

Laurel Leaves & Waves - A Continuous Design

This quilt motif offered a wonderful wave and leaf design perfect for making a continuous design and stitching a "chest band." A wide variety of embroidery motifs lend themselves to creating this sporty look.

The EnVision Clothsetter III is a clever tool that makes it easy to align the motifs for continuous designs. In all the other garments I did not hoop the fleece, but for this application I needed to hoop the fleece to get perfect alignment for the motif continuation.

1. Spray a piece of permanent stabilizer and adhere it to the wrong side of the fleece behind the entire embellishment area.

2. Draw a horizontal line on the fleece for a guideline and plan the motif placement.

3. Hoop the stabilized fleece and stitch the first motif.

4. Using the Clothsetter III, align the second motif and hoop the stabilized fleece.

5. Repeat for the third motif.

6. Trim the excess stabilizer 1/4" away from the outer stitching lines. (Don't trim too closely or it may pull away when inserting the yarn.)

7. Using a blunt-end tapestry needle, insert a double strand of yarn in the channels. Clip the ends of the yarn close to the entry and exit holes. Refer to page 87. Do not stuff the leaves.

8. Pintuck the fleece for a Polar Ribbing neckband. Refer to page 45.

Solitary Rose Pullover

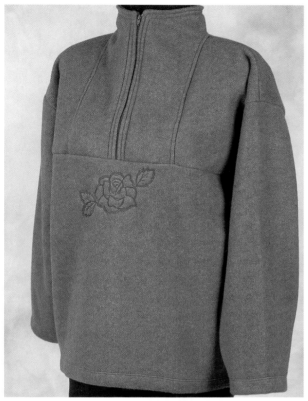

Design from Brother Pacesetter Card #29, "Lace Designs."

I was looking for a bold, stark, single motif to play up this gorgeous dusky heather color. I fell in love with this simple lace rose. Since there are quite a few open areas to stuff, instead of inserting stuffing, I used batting and the "Cheater's" Trapunto method. Couldn't be much easier!

1. Hoop the stabilizer and spray with adhesive.

2. Adhere a piece of low loft batting.

3. Spray the batting with adhesive and adhere the wrong side of the fleece to the batting.

4. Stitch the motif.

5. Trim the excess batting and stabilizer away from the outer edges of the motif.

"It's a Keeper" Pullover

Motif from Brother Pacesetter, "Outrageous Outlines."

Outdoor or sports motifs provide opportunities to embroider for the men in your life. The procedure for adding depth to this design was the same batting technique used in the Solitary Rose Pullover.

I was in the mood to make my own all-over print and this cutwork embroidery motif made it very easy. The design was programmed to stop after the initial outline stitching. It presumed that I was going to cut away the flower petals and prepare for cutwork finishing. Instead, I slit the stabilizer backing, inserted a bit of stuffing, and finished with the satin stitching. I did not stuff the center of the flower to create more depth in the middle of each flower.

All-Over Print Pullover

Motif from Elna EnVision embroidery Card #107, "Cutwork."

Chapter 9
Embossing, stamping, & Embellishing Fleece

Guest Chapter by Dana Bontrager

Nancy's Introduction

When readers asked me to include a chapter on techniques for stamping and embossing fleece, I immediately asked Dana Bontrager to write a guest chapter. Dana is the industry expert on embossing and ink stamping so it was only logical to go directly to the best source for the best information.

Dana is the owner and creative talent behind Purrfection Artistic Wearables and Paw Prints Pattern Co. Since 1984 Dana has made a career of "thinking outside the fashion box." Her focus is on creating unique things to wear. She began designing classy patterns that allow the sewer to be creative and at the same time express individuality. Pretty soon Dana expanded into stamping. And ink-blotting. And resist-and-release dyeing. And embossing. "Printing" on fabric to complement her great patterns.

Not finding enough unique stamps, she bought Pelle's See Thru Stamps so she could design exactly what she wanted. Dana (and her companies) spends her life offering us a wardrobe that is casually simple and wonderfully imaginative.

At first glance you wouldn't think fleece would lend itself to being stamped. Generally, textured fabrics don't make the best choices for a stamped image. But fleece has unique qualities that allow you to create unusual designs and free you from the normally expected results. Not all fleece is alike, so testing and making samples is the best way to discover what's best for the fleece you're working with.

Paints

Textile paints are the medium of choice for stamping, stenciling, and painting fleece. They allow the fabric to be washed without losing the color or the image. Textile paints are also more elastic and flexible, keeping the hand of the fabric as close to the original as possible. There are textile mediums available on the market to add to nontextile paints, but I prefer paints designed specifically for fabric. They are softer and wear longer.

All textile paints vary in some form. Some are heavier, some more liquid. Some dry stiffer than others. Whatever kind you use, it is more than likely you will need to heat set it. Heat setting is required to maintain the color and vibrancy during washing. Fleece requires a different method of heat setting than normally flat fabrics. Because of the nature of the fleece, you wouldn't want to iron the painted images and risk crushing the pile of the fabric. Fleece also cannot take the high heat needed to set most paints thoroughly. Using a blow dryer or heat gun (used commonly by paper stampers) to set the paint is the easiest method. A heat gun should always be tested. They can reach high degrees of heat that may damage the fabric. A blow dryer is a good choice, especially if you have a diffuser attached to it to keep the fabric from blowing away. Set it for the highest (hottest) setting. This is rarely too hot for fabric, but always test to be sure.

Tools

Blank foam pad and foam brayer

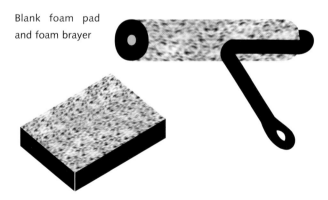

Once you've picked out your paint, the next step is getting it on the fabric. Stamping can be done with a blank foam pad that has been loaded with paint. There are reusable ones available that can be washed out and loaded with another color. You can also use a foam brayer. This tool allows you to apply the paint to a flat nonporous surface (like a plastic pie plate), roll through it to apply the paint to the brayer, then roll across your stamp. It's like having a stamp pad on wheels! There are many advantages to using a foam brayer. You can easily mix colors on a flat plastic surface (often achieving multicolored effects) and you are not limited by the size of a pad (the brayer rolls wherever you want it). You can also apply paint more heavily, which is often what is needed for textured fabrics.

Stenciling on textured fabric is best done with a dense foam sponge. You can use scraps of upholstery foam, makeup wedges, or any foam that is smooth and dense. Don't use kitchen sponges, as they have too many holes where your paint will pool and come out as blobs on your fabric. I like to make my own stencil tool using a scrap of upholstery foam and a bit of string. You can make a firm tool that doesn't bounce and you won't get cramped hands from holding onto a wad of sponge.

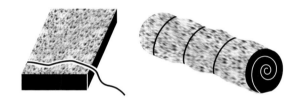

Start with a piece of sponge, about 3" x 3", and a 10" length of string. Lay the string at one edge of the sponge and roll it up tight so it's a cylindrical piece of firm sponge. Wrap the remaining string around it to hold it closed. Tuck the excess string inside to keep it out of the way. Now you have a great little tool that is firm and doesn't bounce. It's shaped like a fat pencil so it's easy to hold, and simple to clean, because you can just unwind the string, undo the sponge, rinse it out, and it will be ready to re-use! The added bonus is that you have two ends to use for different colors of paint!

Additional tools to have on hand are: baby wipes for clean up during a project; a water spray mister to dampen the fleece for heat embossing; plastic spoons to help remove heavier paints from jars and to mix colors, and an old toothbrush to clean the stamps after the work is done.

Stamps

Stamps to emboss fleece must have deeply etched images. This means the image has to be higher than the mount and any background rubber so it will make a clear image. It is also best to use images that are bold and simple (not too detailed). Fleece has a texture, and small or detailed images will just not show up.

Stamps most commonly come in two forms, red (or gray) rubber and photo polymer. Photo polymer stamps are generally clear (although they are sometimes tinted), and are made with a different process than traditional rubber stamps. Neither rubber or photo polymer are sensitive to the heat a home iron can generate for the 30 to 40 seconds it is used to emboss. What is sensitive is the foam pad cushion between a rubber stamp and its wood mount. After time, the heat generated from embossing can break down this foam pad and it will disintegrate. If using wood-mounted rubber stamps, take this into consideration. Photo polymer stamps are usually mounted on clear acrylic mounts without the need for the cushion, so there is nothing to break down from the heat. The most a photo polymer stamp will do is become yellowed from repeated use during heat embossing. This does not affect its usability.

Foam stamps, often used for home décor, should not be used for heat embossing. Plastic stamps also cannot be used, although these are not as commonly found. Wood, metal, or wire images can be used as long as they meet the criterion of a deep image. Special care must be used with metal or wire images. Metals heat up faster and retain the heat more than rubber and you run the risk of scorching your fabric (not to mention your fingers). Always test first.

Stencils

Stencils come in a variety of designs and materials. Most common are the plastic or Mylar stencils available in craft and fabric shops. Look for stencils that are made from a transparent material. It's nice to be able to see your background when placing an image, but it's not totally necessary.

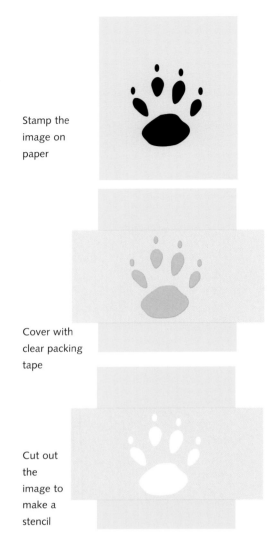

Stamp the image on paper

Cover with clear packing tape

Cut out the image to make a stencil

You can also make your own stencils. These can either be cut from Mylar or template plastic. For a quick project, I make mine from paper and packing tape. Trace or stamp your design on heavy paper or card stock, leaving at least a 2" border around the image. Cover the design with clear packing tape (both sides of the paper should be covered for longest lasting stencil). Cut out the design, using a craft knife. You can use scissors but your edges may not be as smooth. Your stencil is now ready to use! One word of caution: Be sure to use designs that don't have any parts that will drop out when the image is cut from the paper. Stencils typically have connecting parts if there is detail within an image. Look closely at your design. Follow it with your finger. Would any of the detail drop out if an outer segment were removed? Either choose another image or make a bridge to connect the parts so all remain to stencil.

Techniques

Heat Embossing

Embossing fleece requires a hot dry iron, a deeply etched image, and a water mister. You can also emboss with a painted image. Embossing fleece is not as dramatic as velvet or other fabrics where the contrast is high after embossing. Fleece is more tone-on-tone and subtle. Paint embossing allows you to have a bolder image with the paint embedded in the embossed image. Since fleece is a synthetic fiber, some varieties are also resistant to being embossed. Always test a sample before planning a large project.

A smooth sole plate on your iron is best. Unfortunately, most irons are designed for steam, so they have vent holes that will also show up when embossing. Using a Teflon pressing sheet helps eliminate this. Small travel irons usually have smooth sole plates, thus making them ideal for embossing. You are only limited by the size of the small iron. Check your stamp against the iron's sole plate. If it fits within the sole plate, it's fine to use. Another place to look is in thrift stores. Sometimes you can get lucky and find an old iron before steam vents were the norm. Always check to see if it works!

The image on a rubber stamp

Apply firm pressure for 30 to 40 seconds

To emboss an image, place the stamp with the rubber side up on your ironing board. Lay the right side of the fleece against the stamp. Mist lightly with water. It should not be wet, only damp. The iron should be set for the maximum heat the fabric can tolerate. I usually work with a cotton setting, but making a test sample is crucial. Each fabric can vary in its response. If using a steam iron, be sure the steam is off. You don't want to release the embossed image with puffs of steam. Position the iron over the fleece-covered stamp. With firm pressure, press the iron straight down onto the stamp and hold it for 30 to 40 seconds. Do not move it around until you have practiced a bit. If the fabric slips, so does your image! This is where it is important to make test samples – not only to regulate the heat, but also to determine the time needed to create an embossed image. Fleece is dense, so it takes longer than some other fabrics. Remove the iron after the desired time. A kitchen timer with a second counter is a lifesaver. It beats being interrupted while trying to count how many seconds you have held the iron. Your image should be embossed into the right side of the fabric. Check for inconsistencies. Is one side higher than another? Are there missing areas? Be sure to hold the iron evenly. Don't rock across the stamp, as this will make your image uneven.

To paint emboss, you will need to apply textile paint to your image, before heat embossing. Apply paint to the stamp and set it *image side up* on your ironing board. Carefully lay the fleece over the stamp. Do not adjust the fabric once you have set it down on the stamp or the paint will smear. Omit misting with water – there is enough moisture in the paint to create the image. With firm pressure, press the iron straight down onto the stamp and hold it for 30 to 40 seconds. Allow it to cool for a few seconds before removing the fleece. Gently pull away the fabric from the stamp. It will stick a bit, but should come off fairly easily. The painted image is now embedded in the fleece. The added advantage is the paint has already been heat set! Clean the paint from the stamp between each embossing with a baby wipe. Otherwise you will get a buildup of paint and have a harder time removing the fabric.

Stamping

Stamping on fleece is a bit different than stamping on flat fabrics. Because of fleece's texture and fine hairy surface, it is not possible to get extremely distinct and opaque images. The paint will first adhere to the nap of the fleece and then to the background. When you lift up the stamp, the nap will follow, creating a shadowy image. It depends on your project, but this soft shadowy imaging can be a great look, especially when combined with other embellishments. Don't let traditional stamping keep you from creating fun projects just because it looks different!

Stenciling

Stenciling allows you to apply more paint and get a more solid and opaque image than stamping. When stenciling fleece it is necessary to use a dense sponge and work with an up and down pouncing method. The nap will first grab the paint, so dragging across it will only cause a mess. When pouncing up and down with a paint-loaded sponge, the nap is forced into the background and a more solid image can be achieved. Stenciling on fleece takes a while to dry. Use a heat gun or blow dryer to speed up the process and heat set the paint at the same time!

Snowflake Vest

Use a paint embossing technique on this wintry fleece vest to create a stunning companion to any wardrobe.

Designed from Paw Prints pattern #1025, "Sahara."

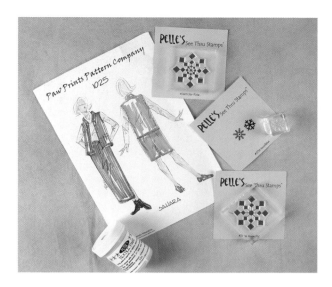

Materials

* 1 yard blue heather fleece (for size small)
* 1/4 yard navy blue cotton
* Moon Flake and Star Flake mini snowflake stamps
* Blue mist pearlescent paint
* Paw Prints pattern #1025 or a similar pattern
* 5 snowflake buttons, 3/4"

Directions

1. From fleece, cut out all the pattern pieces except the placket and one collar stand. Cut the placket and collar stand from cotton.

2. Mark the placement for the snowflakes with pins on the wrong side of the fleece fronts and back. When working with the fronts, lay them side-by-side for an even placement.

3. Apply pearlescent paint to the larger snowflake stamps. Paint emboss the snowflakes into the fleece, alternating each of the two designs in a random pattern. (Refer to paint embossing directions on page 105.)

4. With pearlescent paint, stamp the hidden placket and under collar with mini snowflakes on navy cotton. (The lightweight cotton makes it easier to construct this collared vest by eliminating some of the bulk. It also offers an area to stamp on a flat surface and combine it with the stamped fleece.)

5. Construct the vest as per the patterns directions, omitting the binding for the armholes. (Fleece can be successfully turned under and stitched for a finished armhole.)

6. Add snowflake buttons in a shimmery silver to complete.

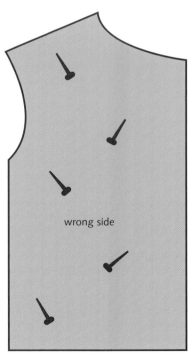

wrong side

Mark snowflake placement with pins

Embossing, Stamping, & Embellishing Fleece ✳ *107*

Curly Cue Long Vest

Combine simple stamping with appliqué to create an unusual calf length vest.

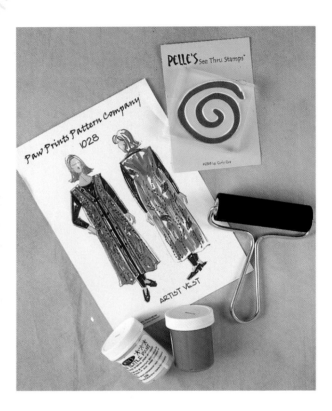

Designed from Paw Prints pattern #1028, "Artist Vest."

Materials
❋ 1-1/2 yards brown heather fleece
❋ 1-1/4 yards boucle fleece
❋ 1 yard plaid cotton trim
❋ Large curly cue stamp
❋ Bronze and gold pearlescent paint
❋ Acrylic sheet
❋ Transparent appliqué sheet
❋ Foam brayer
❋ Paw Prints pattern #1028 or a similar pattern
❋ 1 spool bronze metallic quick bias trim
❋ Rayon thread to match
❋ Clover Mini Iron

Directions

1. Cut out the front and back panels of the vest from brown heather fleece. Cut the sides and front band from boucle fleece.

2. Mix bronze and gold pearlescent paint on an acrylic sheet.

3. Apply the paint mixture to the large curly cue stamp, using a foam brayer.

4. Stamp the front and back vest panels in a dense pattern. (Refer to stamping directions on page 106.)

Metallic bias curly cues applied on top

Curly cues stamped close together on fleece

dana's hint

Once you make the first curly cue, the metallic bias will have left a thin paper divider behind. Use this length to pre-cut the bias strips for more appliqués. It's easier to work with a cut length than the whole roll of bias. Using the Mini Iron protects the nap of the fleece because the tiny soleplate offers precise contact.

5. Make the appliqué curly cues from bronze metallic bias trim. Pre-make each curly cue using the stamped image as a template (you can either stamp one on paper or use the original packaging from the stamp). With a transparent appliqué sheet over the design, use the Clover Mini Iron to apply the metallic bias directly onto the sheet, using the curly cue as a template. Turn under the ends. Allow to cool, and remove from the sheet. The metallic bias curly cues are now pre-formed motifs and much easier to apply to the garment (and more accurate, too!).

6. Arrange the pre-made curly cues on the vest fronts and back. Fuse in place (another good use for the Mini Iron, as your fleece will not get scorched using this smaller tool).

7. Make the appliqués permanent by stitching with a double needle and bronze rayon thread.

8. Construct the vest.

9. Add plaid cotton trim to the front band and armhole edges.

Dalmatian Jacket

*P*lay up the printed fleece with a self-made stencil to make this cute cozy jacket.

Designed from Paw Prints pattern #1009, "Catch the Wave."

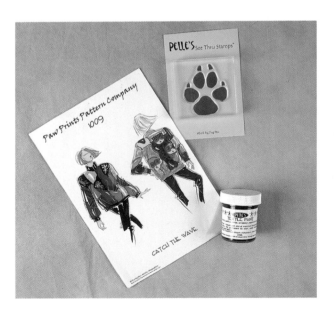

Materials
❋ 1-1/4 yards Dalmatian print fleece
❋ 1-1/4 yards white Nordic fleece
❋ Big dog paw stamp (used to make stencil)
❋ Black paint
❋ Paw Prints pattern #1009 or a similar pattern
❋ 30" zipper (or size to fit)
❋ 1/8 yard black cotton (zipper trim)

Directions
1. First make your own stencil using either the big dog paw stamp, or personalize your jacket using your own dog's paw. Transfer the dog paw onto paper and make your stencil (see page 104).

2. Cut out the jacket front and back panels from white fleece.

3. Use pins to mark the placement for the paw prints on the right side of the fabric. Space the paws one slightly in front of the other, the way an animal actually walks.

4. Stencil the dog paws running up the fronts and down the back of the jacket. (Refer to the stenciling directions on page 106.) Periodically check the back of your stencil. Some paint may bleed to the back. If so, clean the stencil with a baby wipe and dry it on a paper towel before proceeding.

5. Cut the side and sleeve pieces from the Dalmatian print fleece.

6. Assemble the jacket as per the pattern instructions. *Note:* I changed the button front to a zipper closure. I used a narrow strip of black cotton to bind the front edges of the white fleece, so it was easy to install the zipper behind it. And it reduced the bulk, too!

Red Leaves Jacket

L̲et the printed fleece be your guide in designing this jacket. It's a great opportunity to combine appliqué with stamping. When wearing, I roll back the lapels to expose the contrast facing.

Designed from Paw Prints pattern #1027, "Kanji Coat."

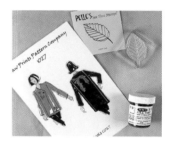

Materials
❋ 2 yards leaf print fleece
❋ 1-1/2 yards black anti-pill fleece
❋ 1/8 yard red linen
❋ Birch leaf stamp
❋ Black paint
❋ Paw Prints pattern #1027 or a similar pattern
❋ 3 buttons, 3/4"

Directions

1. Cut approximately 24 red linen 3" squares. Stamp a black birch leaf inside each square. (Refer to the stamping directions on page 106.) Heat set the stamped linen prior to applying them to the jacket.

2. Cut the fronts and back of the jacket from black fleece. Place the stamped squares on the jacket fronts and back in a random pattern. Appliqué the squares in place by sewing 1/4" away from the raw edge. (You can use a short straight stitch or a ladder-type stitch.) Fringe the edges of each square by pulling the threads of the linen just to the stitching.

3. From leaf print fleece, cut out the rest of the pieces as per the pattern cutting layout.

4. Assemble the jacket, following the pattern instructions, omitting the binding and ignoring the reference to a lapel button.

5. Instead of binding the fleece, finish the edges with a large blanket stitch (by machine or hand), using heavy buttonhole twist thread.

Blue Fern Duster

A̲n enlargement of a fern stamp was used to the create reverse appliqué on this duster coat.

Designed from Paw Prints pattern #1002, "To Dye for Duster."

Materials

* 2 yards blue leaf print fleece
* 1-1/2 yards coordinate solid navy fleece
* 1-1/2 yards blue sueded rayon
* Fern leaf stamp (used for enlarged appliqué)
* Paw Prints pattern #1002 or a similar pattern

Directions

1. Cut out the fronts and back from both navy fleece and blue rayon. Cut the sleeves, facing, and collar from the leaf print fleece.

2. Use a copy machine to enlarge the fern stamp image by 650% for a template. Trace the fern template onto the wrong side of the rayon, spacing the large ferns in a random pattern. (Optional: Stamp tone-on-tone ferns on the wrong side of the rayon around the traced large ferns. This offers additional visual impact to the inside of your coat.)

3. Pin the right side of the rayon to the wrong side of the navy fleece fronts and back. From the rayon side, stitch around the outline and stem of the traced ferns. Carefully trim just the fleece layer from the interior of the large ferns. Trim close to the stitching line, being careful not to snip the rayon underlayer.

4. Assemble the duster, following the pattern instructions.

The lining fabric becomes the fern when using the Reverse Appliqué technique.

Chapter 10
Fleece for the Home

*F*leece is the perfect choice for warm, cozy home accessories like pillows and blankets. Fleece is easy to sew, and easy to care for. Excellent for family rooms, dorms, boats, day care, and retirement homes. Fleece is a great fabric for floor pillows, whether you are curling up in front of the fireplace or cuddling with kids watching television. Pillows and blankets can be as simple or as embellished as fits your taste and home. Color coordinate to accent your home, or combine a variety of leftover scraps from previous projects.

Do you have more fleece leftovers than you have need for blankets? Make blankets and donate them to a homeless shelter or church project to help the less fortunate. Look at Pati's Auction Quilt on page 137 and Marj's Scrap Quilt on page 138 for a couple great ideas to get you started.

Blankets can be any size you want. The size may be determined by the end use, the amount of fleece you have on hand, or it can be influenced by the size of the person who will be using it. A six foot tall college football player obviously needs more "coverage" for his television blanket than a preschooler does for a quiet time "blankie" or a senior does for a wheelchair lap blanket. If you want a blanket sized differently than pictured here, simply "do the math" and alter the yardage needs accordingly.

Look beyond what's pictured. I offer a wide variety of blankets and pillows showing different techniques and looks. The adult-size blankets can be made smaller and with different colors to quickly become kid blankets. Kid blankets, made larger and with adult themes, quickly become grown-up. Don't limit yourself to exactly what is pictured.

Although most of the ideas presented here are shown as blankets and pillows, don't hesitate to take these ideas a couple steps further. Perhaps you need a head rest or arm cover to camouflage worn spots on a favorite old chair. Or a cozy table runner. Or a table-protector for plants.

Blankets – Blankets – Blankets

Quick Fringe Rag Time Quilt

Combine the charm of quilting with the ease of fleece and you have a winning combination. The inspiration for this idea came from Sandy Brawner, owner of Quilt Country in Lewisville, Texas. Sandy designed the popular Rag Time Quilt pattern, which features frayed edges between flannel quilt squares. This is my fleece version.

This is my "fleece version" of the original flannel Rag Time Quilt pattern.

Directions are given here for a two-layer two-color quilt featuring blunt edge reverse appliqué. Single layer one-color or two-color quilt variations are given at the end of these directions.

For the Quick Fringe Rag Time Quilt, the squares are cut 4" larger than the finished inner dimension of the sewn quilt blocks. For 8" quilt squares, the beginning square will be cut 12" x 12". This gives "grace room" for any misalignments or skimpy cuts. You will Quick Fringe the outer 2" and then trim. The outer fringe of the blanket will be trimmed to 1-1/2" and the fringe between the squares will be trimmed to 1".

nancy's note

I chose 12" as the starting size for the squares because the 60" fleece width is evenly divisible by 12, giving the most efficient use of the fabric. However, the starting squares can easily be larger or smaller. Adjust as necessary if your fleece is not a full usable 60" (most are), or if you are working with scraps.

Since you will trim the fringe, you may wonder why you don't just start with shorter fringe. First, it's harder to Quick Fringe short lengths. Second, you will get a clean, even finish when you trim the longer fringe to the exact length you need.

Yardage Requirements for 60" Fleece
❋ Lap quilt: 40" x 56" (excluding fringe)
❋ Color #1: 2-1/3 yards (see Nancy's Hint)
❋ Color #2: 2-1/3 yards (see Nancy's Hint)

nancy's hint

I add 1/3 yard to the above requirements as a "fudge factor." The 2-1/3 yards represents exact needs. The extra 1/3 yard gives a little extra fleece to test the Quick Fringe technique, to test the appliqué, and also allows room for a goof or two (we all have them). Besides, the "leftovers" give you enough to make a coordinating pillow!

Materials
❋ Thread to match Color #1
❋ Thread to match Color #2
❋ Size 90/14 universal needle
❋ Size 100/16 universal needle

Directions
1. Cut 35 12" squares from both colors of fleece.

2. Place all the Color #1 squares in a pile, *right side up.* (To find the right side of the fleece, gently pull along the cut edges, testing both grains for the direction of the most stretch. Choose the edge with the most stretch and gently pull. The fleece will curl towards the wrong side.)

3. Place all the Color #2 squares in a pile, *wrong side up.*

4. Transfer the motifs on pages 118-119 onto the right side of the Color #1 squares - putting the tree motif on the center of 18 squares and the bear/mountain motif on 17 squares. Use one of the transfer techniques outlined in Chapter 3.

5. Alternating a Color #1 traced square and a Color #2 square, place all the squares in pairs, *wrong sides together* (the motifs and right side of Color #2 facing out).

6. Thread a 90/14 needle with Color #1 thread and place Color #2 thread in the bobbin.

7. Place the first fleece pair on your machine, with the Color #1 (traced) fleece facing up.

8. Attach a quilt bar to your machine, placing the guide 2" away from the needle. (If you don't have a quilt bar, place a piece of masking tape to mark the 2" distance from your needle.)

9. Using a 3.5mm stitch length, backtack and begin sewing 2" from one corner, sewing a 2" seam allowance. Stop 2" shy of the edge of the square and pivot to sew the second side at a

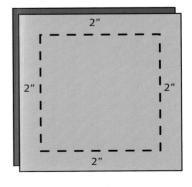

2" seam allowance. Repeat until you arrive back at the starting point. Backtack to secure the stitches.

10. Repeat Steps 8 and 9, sewing all the 35 fleece pairs.

11. Cut out 2" corner squares on all the sewn fleece pairs.

12. Quick Fringe the 2" seam allowances on all the sewn fleece pairs with skimpy 1/2" wide cuts. (Test on a sewn scrap of fleece to see how close to fold over and cut the fringe without cutting the stitching line. Since you will later trim most of the fringe to 1", you want the fringe to be cut close to the stitching line.)

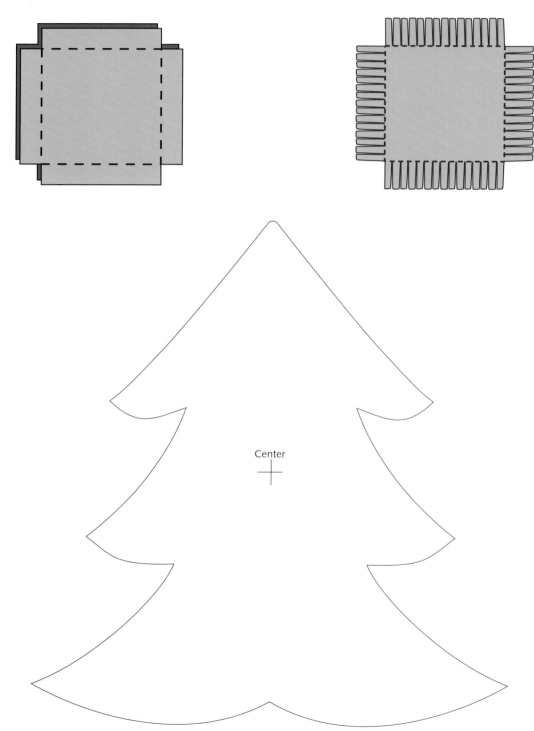

Center

13. Reverse appliqué:

a. With the main color facing up, straight stitch the transferred motif using a 3mm stitch length, securing the stitches at the beginning and end. (Since you are simply straight stitching the motif, there is no need to stabilize the fleece.)

b. Using appliqué or embroidery scissors, trim away the top layer of Color #1 from the inside of the trees to reveal the contrast fleece. Then trim the top layer of Color #2 from the inside of the bear/mountain motifs to reveal the contrast color fleece. Trim close to the stitching line.

nancy's note

For a refresher on the Quick Fringe technique, refer to page 59.

Center

Note: Pay careful attention to the following directions for trimming the fringe and sewing the squares together. The end result is a blanket made up of alternating color squares, with four layers of 1" fringe sticking up between all the squares, and two layers of 1-1/2" fringe finishing the perimeter.

14. Prepare to trim the fringe and sew the squares together by arranging the squares according to the illustration (see Nancy's Fringe Hint).

15. Trim the fringe to 1-1/2" on those edges that will be the outer edges of the quilt (see Nancy's Fringe Hint).

16. Trim the fringe to 1" on those sides of the squares that will be sewn to another square (see Nancy's Fringe Hint).

17. Change to a 100/16 needle. When sewing the square together, you are sewing through four layers of fleece, and need a larger needle.

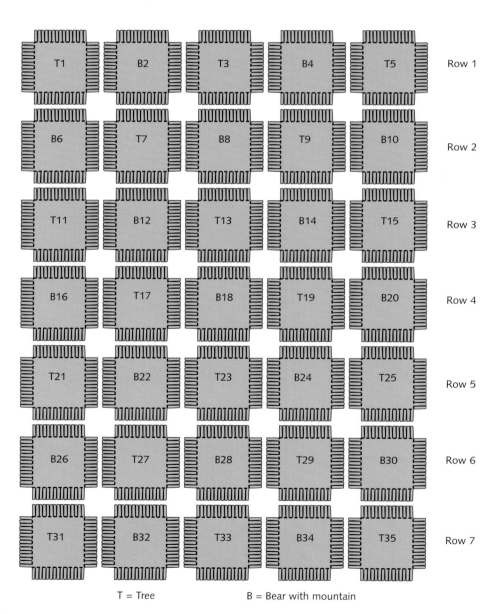

T1	B2	T3	B4	T5	Row 1
B6	T7	B8	T9	B10	Row 2
T11	B12	T13	B14	T15	Row 3
B16	T17	B18	T19	B20	Row 4
T21	B22	T23	B24	T25	Row 5
B26	T27	B28	T29	B30	Row 6
T31	B32	T33	B34	T35	Row 7

T = Tree   B = Bear with mountain

nancy's fringe hint

I found it easiest (and least subject to error) to first lay out the entire quilt on a table. Then I used pins to mark all the outer edges that were to have 1-1/2" fringe. I then worked on one row at a time, working my way down the quilt as follows:

Top row:

a. Cut all the pin-marked edges to 1-1/2" fringe.

b. Cut the unmarked edges to 1" fringe.

c. Sew the squares *wrong sides together* with fringe exposed between the squares.

d. Repeat for the rest of the rows, cutting the pin-marked edges to 1-1/2" and unmarked edges to 1".

e. Sew the rows together to complete the quilt.

18. Referring to the numbers in the illustration, sew square T1 to square B2 with *wrong* sides together. Four layers of 1" fringe are exposed on the right side of the blanket, between the squares. (The wrong side of the blanket looks like an ordinary seam.) Sew squares together using a 3.5mm stitch length, being careful not to catch any fringe in the seamline.

19. Repeat Step 18, sewing B2 to T3, to B4, to T5, completing Row 1. (Double check: 1-1/2" fringe on the left, upper, and right sides of Row 1, 1" fringe between squares and at the lower edge of the row.)

20. Repeat Steps 18 and 19 to sew Row 2 through Row 6. (Double check: 1-1/2" fringe on the left and right sides of each row, 1" fringe between squares and at the upper and lower edges of the row.)

21. Repeat Steps 18 and 19 to sew Row 7. (Double check: 1-1/2" fringe on the left, lower, and right edges, 1" fringe between squares and at the upper edge.)

22. Sew the top row to the second row, wrong sides together, having four layers of fringe exposed on the right side. Match the seamlines and be careful not to catch the fringe in the stitching.

23. Sew the remaining horizontal rows together to complete the quilt.

Single Layer Two-Color Quick Fringe Rag Time Quilt

(Takes you as long to say it as it does to sew it!)

D o you like the checkerboard effect but only want one layer of fleece? Make the Single Layer Quick Fringe Quilt from two solid colors of fleece, or a print and a solid color.

Yardage Requirements for 60" Fleece
❋ Color #1: 1-1/3 yards
❋ Color #2: 1-1/3 yards

Directions
1. Cut 18 12" squares of Color #1 and cut 17 12" squares of Color #2.

2. Refer to the construction instructions for the Quick Fringe Rag Time Quilt (page 117). For this quilt, you are fringing and piecing a single layer of fleece instead of double layers.

nancy's note
There will be enough extra yardage to test the Quick Fringe Technique. However, add a little extra yardage if you want appliqués in some of the squares.

Single Layer One-Color Quick Fringe Rag Time Quilt

This quilt is also very pretty when done with only one color. Obviously one layer eliminates the use of reverse appliqué. But if appliqué is desired, consider using a simple blunt edge appliqué.

Yardage Requirements for 60" Fleece
❋ 2 -1/3 yards (see Nancy's Hint)

Directions
1. Cut 35 12" squares.

2. Refer to the construction instructions for the Quick Fringe Rag Time Quilt (page 117). For this quilt, you are fringing and piecing a single layer of fleece instead of double layers.

nancy's hint

The yardage given is exact. Personally, I add a little extra to test the Quick Fringe technique.

Double Border Blankets & Coordinating Pillows

This blanket is so quick and easy to make that it can be finished without even turning on your sewing machine! Fleece double border prints offer dramatic looks and lend themselves beautifully to home dec use.

Motifs from Cactus Punch, Nancy Cornwell's "Adventures With Fleece" design pack.

Yardage Requirements for 60" Fleece
❋ Decide the size of blanket you want. Generally 1-1/2 to 2 yards

Directions
1. Finish the edges in one of the following manners:

a. Blunt edge finish: Using a rotary cutter, trim the selvage edges and Quick Fringe the crossgrain ends with 4" fringe. Just like that and you are finished!

b. Serger finish the edges with a coarse thread or yarn.

c. Back the fleece with another layer of fabric (fleece, cotton, flannel, denim) and finish using traditional quilting techniques.

Double Border Coordinate Pillows

Study the border and decide what part you want to accent. On the Forest Pillow, the trees were placed so as to leave a bit of sky visible for embellishment with tone-on-tone embroidered birds.

The Mountain Scene offered more choices. One pillow is scenic, featuring the tree, while the other pillow uses the sky portion of the print and is embellished with embroidered snowflakes.

(Refer to the Sunflower Pillow on page 142 and Trapunto Sampler Pillow on page 147 for pillow construction directions.)

What's Trump? –
Double Reverse Appliqué Blanket

Whether for the game room or family room, this blanket is sure to please any card-playing enthusiast. For coordinating fleece coasters, buy an extra 1/8 yard of each color. Straight stitch the spade, heart, diamond, and club motifs onto double-layered fleece, trim one layer, then rotary trim finish.

Yardage Requirements for 60" Fleece
Blanket size: 40" x 56" (excluding fringe)
✳ Black: 1-1/4 yards
✳ Red: 1-1/4 yards
✳ Thread: black, red
✳ Size 90/14 universal needle

Directions
1. Trim the selvages from both fleeces.

2. Place the black fleece against the red fleece wrong sides together.

3. Sew the fleece layers together with a 2" seam allowance, pivoting at the corners. The needle thread should be the same color as the top fleece color and the bobbin thread should match the bottom fleece. Using a 3.5mm stitch length, backtack and begin sewing 2" from one corner, sewing a 2" seam allowance. Stop 2" shy of the edge of the blanket and pivot to sew the second side at a 2" seam allowance. Repeat until you arrive back at the starting point. Backtack to secure the stitches.

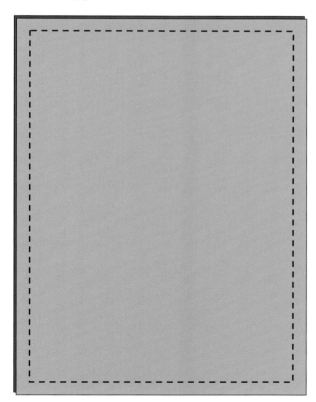

4. Mark and straight stitch lines to form a grid, 5 squares x 7 squares. The squares will be approximately 8" x 8". As a double check, measure the inner blanket dimension (between seamlines) and divide into a 5 x 7 block grid. Adjust the square sizes as necessary.

S	H	C	D	S
H	C	D	S	H
C	D	S	H	C
D	S	H	C	D
S	H	C	D	S
H	C	D	S	H
C	D	S	H	C

S = Spade   C = Club
H = Heart   D = Diamond

5. Transfer the spade, heart, diamond, and club motifs from page 129 to the centers of the squares, using one of the transfer techniques outlined in Chapter 3 and referring to the illustration for motif placement. Carefully follow the sequence so you alternate red and black suits. (Bridge players be careful: The suits are by alternating color rather than rank order.)

6. Straight stitch the transferred motifs using a 3.0mm stitch length, securing the stitches at the beginning and end. The needle thread should be the same color as the top fleece color and the bobbin thread should match the bottom fleece.

7. Using appliqué or embroidery scissors, neatly trim away the top red layer from the spade and club motifs to reveal the black fleece. Neatly trim away the top black layer from the heart and diamond motifs to reveal the red fleece. Trim close to the stitching.

jeff's note

It's not a bad idea to mark the center of each motif that is going to be trimmed away. This helps eliminate the possibility of cutting out the wrong side.

nancy's comments regarding jeff's note

That is the voice of experience speaking. Jeff, my husband, graciously trimmed the motifs while I sewed and wrote. He felt this was definitely a hint worth mentioning.

8. Cut out 2" corner squares at all four blanket corners.

S	H	C	D	S
H	C	D	S	H
C	D	S	H	C
D	S	H	C	D
S	H	C	D	S
H	C	D	S	H
C	D	S	H	C

9. Quick Fringe the 2" seam allowances with skimpy 1/2" wide cuts.

S	H	C	D	S
H	C	D	S	H
C	D	S	H	C
D	S	H	C	D
S	H	C	D	S
H	C	D	S	H
C	D	S	H	C

nancy's note

For a refresher on the Quick Fringe technique, refer to page 59.

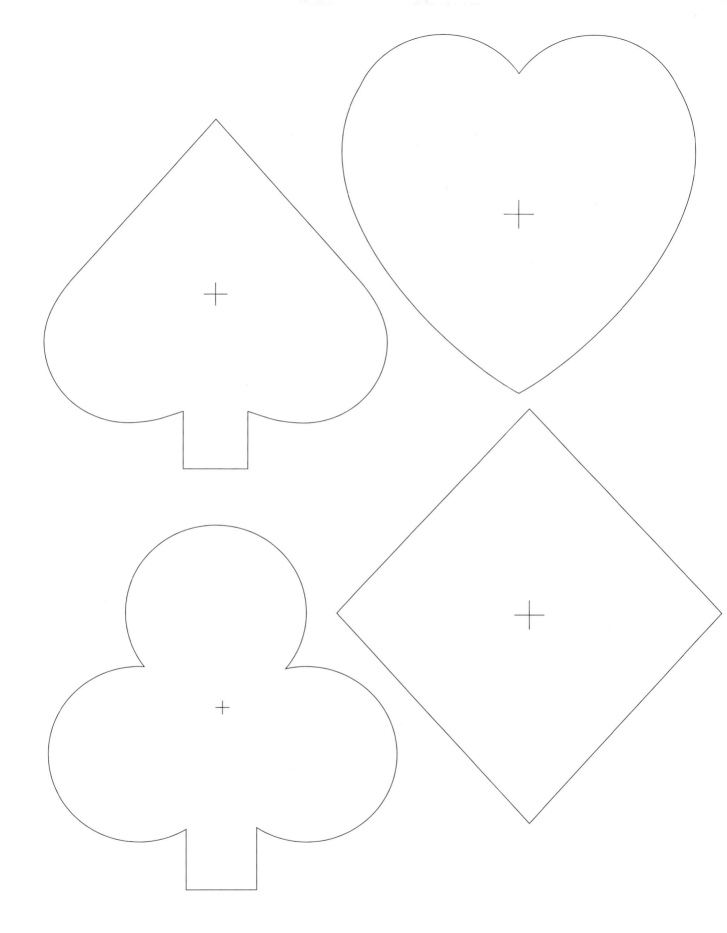

Double Reverse Appliqué Quilt

Prefer quilting to card playing? Take Marj Ostermiller's lead and make a double reverse appliqué blanket using popular quilt motifs. Stitch the motif, and trim different sections from opposite sides. The family member who loves pink can cuddle with the pink side facing up, while the person who loves the drama of black can curl up with the black side facing out.

Blanket made by Marj Ostermiller.

Print Reverse Appliqué Blanket

Team a dynamic print fleece with a coordinate solid fleece. Outline stitch parts of the print to serve as the motifs for the reverse appliqué. Use the extra yardage to make coordinating pieces for the baby.

Yardage Requirements for 60" Fleece
❋ Print: 1 to 1-1/2 yards
❋ Solid: 1 to 1-1/2 yards
❋ Thread to match both colors
Note: Purchase yardage according to how large a blanket you want and if you plan to make any coordinating accessories or garments. A blanket can be as small as 36" x 36" (pretty small) to 36" x 45" (nice size) to 45" x 54" (generous size).

Directions
1. Cut both fleeces to the size blanket you wish to make.

2. Place fleeces *wrong sides together.*

3. Sew the blanket together around the entire outer edge using one of the edge finishes suggested in the Double Reverse Appliqué Baby Blanket, page 132.

4. Place the blanket on your machine, *print side facing up.* Straight stitch the various elements of the fleece print using a 3mm stitch length. The needle thread should be the same color as the top fleece (print) color and the bobbin thread should match the bottom (solid) fleece. Avoid tiny motifs. If necessary, exaggerate the size by outline stitching larger than the actual motif size. (Since you are simply straight stitching the motif, there is no need to stabilize the fleece.)

5. Use appliqué or embroidery scissors to trim away the solid color fleece layer close to the stitching line, to reveal the dynamic print.

Double Reverse Appliqué Baby Blanket

*L*ove both baby colors of your fleece and having a hard time declaring one of them to be the "right" side? Sprinkle baby motifs and do double reverse appliqué. (Obviously you won't trim away from the same motif on both sides or else you will end up with unintentional cutwork!) Since you do not need to use the full 60" width of the fleece for a tiny baby, take advantage of the extra width to make a coordinating pullover fleece top, cuddly fleece pants, a precious little hat, or little stuffed toy.

Yardage Requirements for 60" Fleece
* Color #1: 1 to 1-1/2 yards
* Color #2: 1 to 1-1/2 yards
* Thread to match both colors

Note: Purchase yardage according to how large a blanket you want and if you plan to make any coordinating accessories or garments. A blanket can be as small as 36" x 36" (pretty small) to 36" x 45" (nice size) to 45" x 54" (generous size).

Directions

1. Cut both colors of fleece to the size blanket you wish to make.

2. Place the fleeces *wrong sides together*.

3. Sew the blanket together around the entire outer edge, using one of the following edge finishing techniques:

a. With thread colors matching the fleeces in the needle and bobbin, straight stitch a seam at 1/2" to 5/8", rounding corners if desired. Trim close to the stitching, using either a straight or wavy rotary blade. When trimming, lay a clear plastic ruler offset from the seamline line to use as a guide.

b. Attach a quilt bar to your machine and set it for a distance 2" to 3" away from your needle. (If you do not have a quilt bar, place a piece of masking tape on the bed of your machine, 2" to 3" away from the needle.) With needle thread matching the top color fleece and bobbin thread matching the bottom color fleece, sew the blanket layers together with a 2" to 3" seamline. Backtack at the beginning and ending. Cut out 2" or 3" squares at the corners. Quick Fringe with 1/2" cuts (see the Quick Fringe directions on page 59). *Important Caution:* Do not cut narrower than 1/2" fringe or else you run the risk of the fringe tearing off and presenting a danger to the baby.

c. Serger edge finish using a yarn matching one of the colors, contrasting with both colors, or a variegated yarn.

4. Transfer very simple baby motifs (easily found in appliqué books, coloring books, wrapping paper, etc.) onto one side of the fleece blanket, using one of the transfer techniques outlined in Chapter 3.

5. Straight stitch the motifs using a 3mm stitch length. The needle thread should be the same color as the top fleece color and the bobbin thread should match the bottom fleece.

6. Using appliqué or embroidery scissors, trim away one fleece layer close to the stitching line, to reveal the underlying layer. Alternate trimming the motifs on both sides. The net result is an arrangement of outline-stitched motifs and trimmed motifs on both sides. (Remember that you can't trim the same motif from both sides or you'll have cutwork!)

Double Appliqué Blanket

*I*n More Polarfleece® Adventures *I introduced the Blunt Edge method of appliqué on fleece. The Blunt Edge finish takes advantage of the nonraveling quality of fleece. Simply cut out shapes from solid or print fleece, lightly spray the wrong side of the fleece appliqués with KK2000, and adhere them to the fleece garment or blanket. Then edge stitch the appliqué in place and, quick as a wink, you are done. But… this blanket offers a bonus - back-to-back appliqués on both sides of the blanket!*

This double layer appliqué idea, a fun variation of the Blunt Edge appliqué technique, comes from Jeanine Twigg (the Snap Source snap expert and author of *It's a Snap*, embroidery expert and author of *Embroidery Machine Essentials*, and lover of sewing with fleece). When Jeanine heard I was writing this book, she sent me this clever idea.

Although I feature this technique in soft pretty baby colors, this idea would work beautifully in many other themes:
* Earthy colors with double appliqué leaves or trees
* Soccer balls, footballs, baseballs, or basketballs sewn in team colors
* Sky blue fleece with stars, clouds, and an occasional crescent moon

Whatever you choose, just remember to keep the motif simple and fairly basic.

Want to venture beyond blankets? This idea would work beautifully on a reversible vest.

Yardage Requirements for 60" Fleece
* 1 to 1-1/2 yards fleece
* Scraps in complementary colors for appliqué
* Thread to match

Directions
Note: Directions are given for both conventional sewing machines and embroidery machines.

1. Cut the fleece to the size blanket you wish to make.

2. Finish the edges with a straight or wavy blade rotary cutter, serger finish using a pretty yarn, or Quick Fringe.

3. Determine the placement of the various motifs with a fabric marker, pencil, or pins. (Need help? See Nancy's Hints at the end of the directions.)

Conventional Sewing Machine Directions
1. For each double appliqué, cut two pieces of fleece for the appliqués at least 2" larger all around than the finished appliqué. For the heart motif given here, the appliqué fleece pieces need to be at least 8" x 8".

2. Draw a heart motif on the right side of one fleece appliqué piece, using one of the transfer techniques outlined in Chapter 3.

3. Lightly spray KK2000 on the wrong side of a traced appliqué piece and adhere it to the blanket at a placement mark.

4. Lightly spray KK2000 on the wrong side of the second appliqué piece (not traced) and adhere it to the opposite side of the blanket, sandwiching the blanket between the appliqué pieces. (This is why the appliqué pieces are larger than you really need. The alignment will not be exact.)

5. Straight stitch the heart motif using a 3mm stitch length. The needle thread should be the same color as the top appliqué piece and the bobbin thread should match the appliqué piece.

6. Using appliqué or embroidery scissors, trim the excess fleece from the outer edges of the stitching on both appliqué pieces, trimming close to the stitching line. (It's worth doing a "test trim" on a sample to find the best angle to hold the scissors for the neatest finish.)

7. Repeat sewing the sets of appliqués until the blanket is embellished as you want.

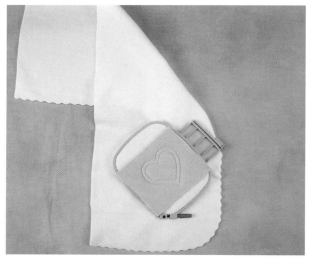

Embroidery Machine Directions
1. Choose a simple outline embroidery motif.

2. For each motif, cut two fleece appliqué pieces at least 2" larger all around than the finished appliqué.

3. Lightly hoop the blanket.

4. Lightly spray KK2000 on the wrong side of one fleece appliqué piece and adhere it to the underside of the hooped blanket, centering the appliqué piece in the stitching area.

5. Lightly spray the wrong side of the second fleece appliqué piece and adhere it to the top side of the hooped blanket, centering it in the stitching area.

6. With thread colors matching the fleece colors in the needle and the bobbin, outline stitch the motif.

7. Using appliqué or embroidery scissors, trim the excess fleece from the outer edges of the stitching on both appliqué pieces, trimming close to the stitching line. (It's worth doing a "test trim" on a sample to find the best angle to hold the scissors for the neatest finish.)

8. Repeat sewing the sets of appliqués until the blanket is embellished as you want.

Pati's Auction Quilt

When Pati Sutton showed me pictures of what she had done with her granddaughter's kindergarten class for their fund-raising auction, I knew there were many sewers who could take advantage of this wonderful idea.

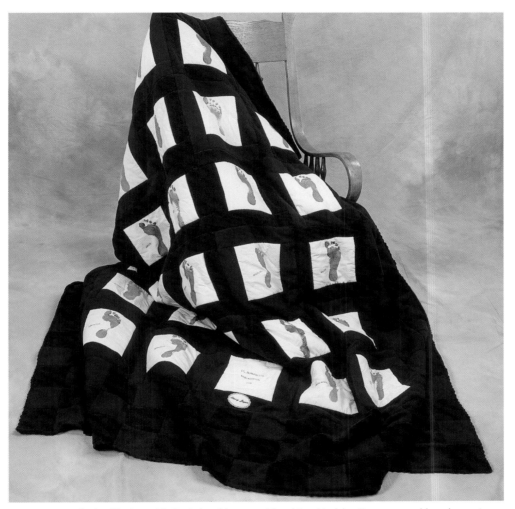

Pati Sutton made this blanket with the help of her granddaughter, Madalyn Freeman, and her classmates.

Using cotton fabric for the center blocks, fuchsia acrylic paint for the girls, and green paint for the boys, Pati had the children imprint their footprint in the center of a square. (What makes me think this was the best part of the quilt as far as the kids were concerned?) Each child's name was then embroidered alongside their footprint.

Pati backed the cotton fabric with cotton batting to balance it to the weight of the fleece. The blocks were sewn together with a straight stitch seam, and then over-sewn with an open serpentine stitch on top to flatten the bulk. You can back the quilt with just about anything: quilting cotton, flannel, fleece, or as Pati's group did... a sheet!

Marj's Scrap Quilt

Looking for a good home for those leftover fleece pieces that are too small for anything yet too large to toss out? Marj Ostermiller scrounged through her fleece scrap pile, pulled out prints that worked well together, and made this charming and very cozy scrap quilt. To make even better use of her "resource center" (high-tech name for fabric stash), she also used up lots of flannel scraps!

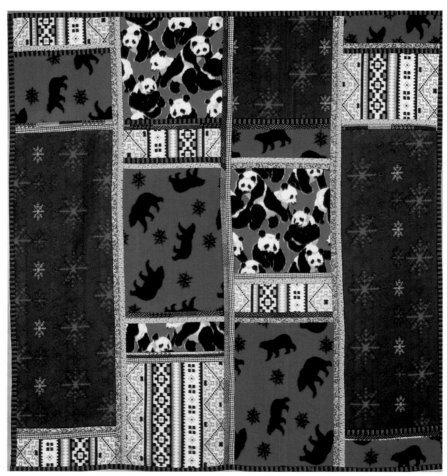

Blanket made by Marj Ostermiller.

After choosing which fleece prints she wanted to use, Marj cut them into squares and rectangles. She sewed the quilt together in sort of a crazy patch fashion. Marj first finished edges of the fleece pieces with flannel binding, then butted the finished sections together and joined them with a universal or serpentine stitch. She finished the outer edge with flannel binding.

It's an easy "design-as-you-go" approach.

Pillows – Pillows – Pillows

Trapunto sampler pillows. Pillows with embroidery framed with chenille. Rag quilt pillows. Border pillows. Flanged edge finishes. Fat Piping edge finish. Quick Fringe edge finish.

Any embellishment that can be done on fleece can be turned into a pillow.

nancy's note

The pillow directions in this chapter include information for specific embellishment techniques and edge finishes. Mix and match techniques to suit your taste. At the end of the Sunflower Pillow and the Quilter's Trapunto Sampler Pillow are directions for adapting to different pillow sizes.

Rag Time Quilt Pillow

Love the Rag Time Blanket and want a coordinating pillow?

Materials
❉ 16" pillow form
❉ Color #1: 2/3 yard
❉ Color #2: 2/3 yard

Directions
1. Construct the pillow front the same as the blanket, using four squares. (The inner fringe is 1" long. Leave the perimeter fringe 2" long for now.)

2. Cut two pillow half backs, 20" x 14".

3. Sew a 2" hem, overlap 4", and baste together. (Refer to Steps #15-17 on page 144.)

4. Cut out 2" corners on the half backs. (Refer to Step #11 on page 118.)

5. Quick Fringe 2" on the half backs. (Refer to Step #12 on page 118.)

6. Sew the pillow front to the pillow half backs, wrong sides together (in finished position), using a 2" seam allowance.

7. Trim the perimeter fringe (three layers) to 1-1/2".

Border Print Pillows

*B*order *fleece prints offer a tremendous opportunity to dress up a room with dramatic throws and coordinating pillows.*

Play up the dramatic features of the print (like the single tall tree) or subtly embellish with hints of embroidery (like the sky sprinkled with snowflakes or birds.)

Finish with either a Fat Piping edge finish (refer to the directions for the Sunflower Pillow on page 142) or the Flanged Edge finish (refer to the directions for the Quilter's Trapunto Sampler Pillow on page 147).

Sunflower Pillow (With Fat Piping Finish)

Featuring "Cheater's" Trapunto and Fat Piping finish.

Materials

* 16" square pillow form
* 5/8 yard mid-weight fleece
* Large decorative button for flower center
* Medium loft batting, 11" x 11"
* 1/3 yard Soft 'n Sheer permanent stabilizer
* Sulky KK2000 temporary adhesive spray
* 4.0/80 or 4.0/100 double needle (for pintucked petals)
* 100/16 universal needle, for construction (see Nancy's Note)
* Spool rayon thread, slightly darker than fleece color

nancy's note

Normally you would use a 14/90 needle for construction. But, when you come to the Fat Piping finish, you will be sewing on four layers of fleece and need the strength of the larger size needle.

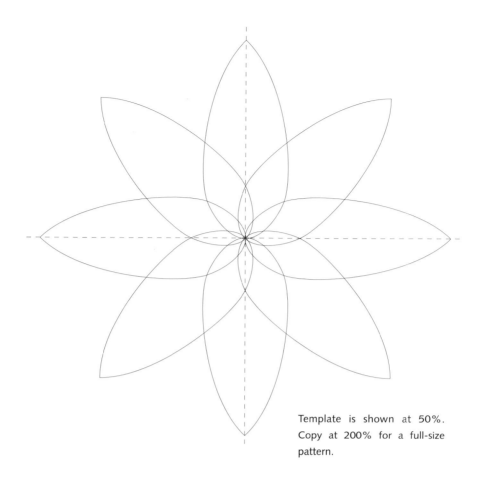

Template is shown at 50%.
Copy at 200% for a full-size
pattern.

Directions

1. For the Fat Piping trim finish, cut one 3" x 60" trim strip on the crossgrain. (If making a 16" pillow and using 58" to 60" fleece, one trim strip should suffice.)

2. Cut the pillow front 19" x 19" (3" larger than the finished pillow size).

3. On right side of the pillow front, draw horizontal and perpendicular lines to mark the exact center.

4. Using the sunflower template, transfer the motif onto the pillow front, centering the design and using your favorite transfer method from Chapter 3.

5. Cut a piece of Soft 'n Sheer permanent stabilizer 11" x 11".

6. Cut a piece of medium loft batting 11" x 11".

7. Lightly spray the stabilizer with KK2000 and adhere the batting.

8. Lightly spray the batting with KK2000 and adhere the wrong side of the fleece pillow front to the batting, centering the traced motif over the batting.

9. Insert a 4.0 double needle and thread both needles with rayon thread. (Wind an extra bobbin with rayon thread and use this bobbin thread for the second needle.) Use regular thread in the bobbin.

10. Begin sewing at the center of the motif. Beginning at the middle of the motif, center the double needles over the drawn motif lines and sew one long continuous pintuck. Stitching always comes back to the middle and loops onto the next petal. Pivot at the petal points. (Most fleece is soft enough to pivot and turn in one step. If the needles balk at pivoting in one step, take a stitch or two to "get around the corner.")

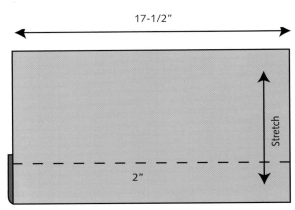

17-1/2"

Stretch

2"

17. Pin the pillow front to the basted pillow half backs, wrong sides together (finished position). Do not stitch yet.

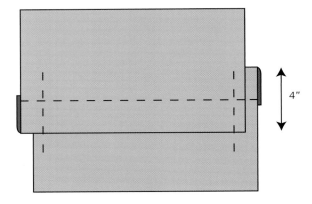

4"

18. Place the right side of the 3" trim strip (from Step #1) against the right side of the pillow front, beginning at a midpoint on the pillow and avoiding the pillow half back overlap area.

19. Using an exact 3/4" seam allowance, begin sewing 4" from one end of the trim strip. (You are

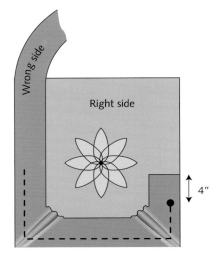

Wrong side

Right side

4"

11. Trim the excess stabilizer and batting close to the stitching.

12. Re-true and trim the pillow front to 17-1/2" x 17-1/2" (1-1/2"larger than the pillow form).

13. Sew a large decorative button at the center of the motif for the sunflower center.

14. From the remaining fleece, cut two pillow half backs 17-1/2" x 12-3/4".

nancy's note

If you have enough fleece and nap is not an issue, cut the 17-1/2" in the degree of the least stretch. Since you are making a flap envelope closing on the backside of the pillow, there is less potential for distortion if it is cut this way.

15. Turn under and topstitch 2" hems on one long edge of each half back.

16. Overlap the half back hems 4" and baste together at 1/2".

sewing through three layers: front, back, and trim strip.)

20. Sew the trim strip to the entire outer edge of the pillow, pivoting at the corners, stopping exactly 4" before the beginning stitching.

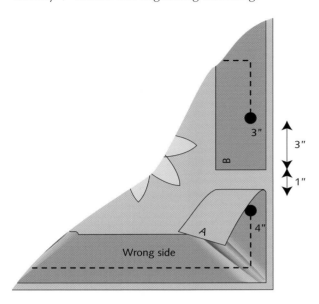

21. Cut the ending edge of the strip exactly 3" beyond the ending stitching.

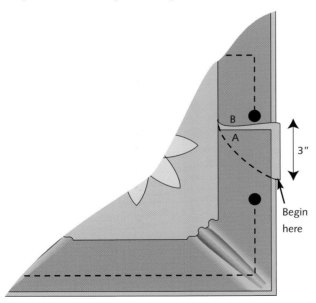

22. Lift up both unsewn ends of the trim strip. Match and pin edge A to edge B, right sides together.

23. Sew A to B "on the diagonal," beginning exactly at corner of B.

24. Before trimming the triangle points from the spliced strip, double check on the right side to make sure everything is correct. Trim the seam allowance to 1/4" and finger press the seam allowance open.

25. Finish sewing the last 4" of the spliced trim strip to the pillow.

26. Trim away *one* layer in the overlap area on the half backs to make the bulk comparable to the rest of the pillow. (Do not trim away any other seam allowance. In the following steps, when wrapping and enclosing the seam allowance, the fluffiness of the fleece "plumps" the wrap and gives a Fat Piping appearance.)

27. To finish the Fat Piping edge, wrap the trim strip to the backside, wrapping up, over, and around, encasing the raw edge seam allowances. You may choose to trim just the tips of the pillow corners for ease in wrapping.

28. Working from the front side of the pillow, pin the trim strip in place, making sure the plump wrapped edges are perfectly even.

29. Using an edge stitch presser foot for precision stitch placement and sewing from the front side of the pillow, stitch-in-the-ditch to secure the wrapped trim strip on the backside. (To stitch-in-the-ditch, sew exactly on the seamline.)

30. On the backside of the pillow, use sharp scissors to cut the excess trim close to the stitching line.

31. Insert the pillow form through the flap opening.

Requirements for Different Size Pillow Forms With Fat Piping Finish

1. For a larger pillow, yardage needed is equal to the pillow dimension plus 9".

2. The beginning pillow front is cut 3" larger than the pillow form – 1-1/2" larger all around (Step #2).

3. After finishing the motif stitching, the pillow is re-trued and cut to 1-1/2" larger than the pillow form – 3/4" larger all around (Step #12).

4. The pillow half backs allow for 2" hems and 4" overlap, finishing 1-1/2" larger than the pillow form.

5. One 3" x 60" trim strip, cut on the crossgrain, is long enough to finish the edge of a 16" or smaller pillow. If making a larger pillow, cut two 3" x 60" trim strips, and splice to make one long strip.

6. Sew the trim to the pillow with an exact 3/4" seam allowance for a finished 7/8" fat piping.

7. Follow the construction directions for the Sunflower Pillow, Steps #17 to 30.

Quilter's Trapunto Sampler Pillow (With Flanged Edge Finish)

Featuring Trapunto and Flanged Edge finish. Directions are given for both a conventional sewing machine and an embroidery machine.

Motifs from Viking Embroidery Disk #101, "Designer Quilt" by Kerstin Widell.

Materials
* 5/8 yard mid-weight fleece
* 14" square pillow form
* 4 quilt motifs, 4" to 5" overall dimension
* 1/3 yard Soft 'n Sheer permanent stabilizer
* Sulky KK2000 temporary adhesive spray
* Small handful polyester stuffing
* 1 spool rayon thread, slightly darker than fleece color
* 90/14 embroidery needle (for motif stitching)
* 90/14 universal needle for construction
* 6.0/100 double needle (for pintuck grid lines)
* Regular thread for construction

Directions
1. Cut the pillow front 19" x 19" (5" larger than the pillow form).

2. On the right side of the pillow front, draw horizontal and vertical lines to mark the exact center. Draw marks on each line 7" away from the center. (This serves as a reference to mark the outer edges of the pillow top.)

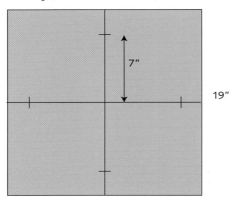

3. Using the double needle and appropriate presser foot, stitch a pintuck row on either side of the drawn horizontal and vertical lines.

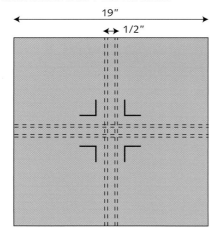

4. Draw marks for the placement of the motifs inside the corners, 1" away from the pintuck grid lines.

5. Prepare the pillow front to stitch motifs as follows:

Embroidery Machine:
a. Choose a hoop larger than indicated. (This allows more freedom to move the motif for alignment purposes.)

b. Hoop Soft 'n Sheer stabilizer. Using a Chacopel pencil, draw horizontal and perpendicular lines on the stabilizer to help with accurate fleece placement.

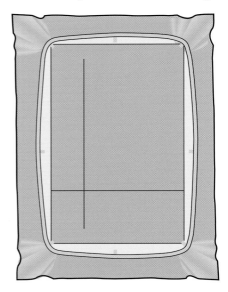

c. Spray the stabilizer with KK2000 temporary adhesive and adhere it to the fleece, aligning the pintuck lines to the lines drawn on the stabilizer. Check the perimeter of the design to make sure the fleece is adhered squarely in the hoop.

Conventional Sewing Machine:
a. Transfer the quilt motifs onto each quadrant, using your favorite transfer method from Chapter 3.

b. Spray the stabilizer with KK2000 temporary adhesive and adhere it to the wrong side of the fleece pillow front.

6. For more noticeable stitching lines, stitch the motif with two strands of rayon thread in the needle.

7. Trim the excess stabilizer close to the stitching lines.

8. For a raised trapunto effect, in the unstitched areas of the motifs, make a small slit in the *stabilizer only*. Lightly stuff and hand stitch the opening closed (see page 89).

9. Trim the pillow front to 18" x 18" (4" larger than the pillow form).

10. Cut two pillow half backs, 18" x 13". (If you have enough fleece and nap is not an issue, cut the pillow half backs with the least amount of stretch going in the 18" direction.)

11. Turn under and topstitch 2" hems on each half back

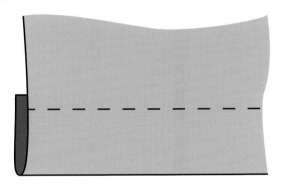

12. Overlap the half back hems 4" and baste them together at 1/2".

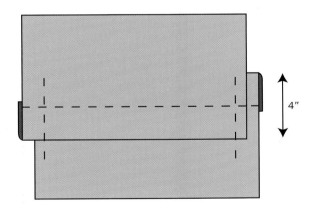

13. With right sides together, pin and stitch the pillow front to the basted pillow half backs using a 1" seam allowance. Do not trim the seam allowance.

14. Trim the corners diagonally.

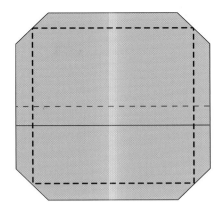

15. Trim one layer from the "overlap area" on the half backs. This makes the bulk comparable to the rest of the pillow.

16. Turn the pillow to the finished position. Arrange the seam allowances to lay flat.

17. Topstitch at 1", creating a 1" flange around the entire pillow.

Requirements for Different Size Pillow Forms With Flanged Edge Finish

1. The beginning pillow front is cut 5" larger than the pillow form – 2-1/2" larger all around (Step #1).

2. After finishing the motif stitching, the pillow is re-trued and cut to 4" larger than the pillow form – 2" larger all around (Step #9).

3. The pillow half backs allow for 2" hems, 4" overlap, and finishing 4" larger than the pillow form – 2" larger all around.

4. Follow the construction directions for the Quilter's Trapunto Sampler Pillow, Steps #13-17.

Chenille Pillow (With Fat Piping Finish)

Chenille can "frame" an embroidery motif, a dramatic appliqué, a trapunto design, or it can stand on its own merit. Directions are given for creating the chenille frame on the pillow top and contrast Fat Piping finish.

Motif from Brother Pacesetter, "Outrageous Outlines."

Materials
❋ 16" pillow form
❋ 5/8 yard mid-weight white 60" wide fleece
❋ 5/8 yard mid-weight black 60" wide fleece
❋ 5/16" Mini Omnistrip cutting mat

Directions
1. For the Fat Piping finish, cut a strip of black fleece 3" x 60" on the crossgrain.

2. Cut a white fleece pillow top 19" x 19" (3" larger than the pillow form).

3. On the right side of the white fleece, draw lines to mark the exact center of the pillow front.

4. Add a center design by embroidering, stitching a quilt motif, sculpture stitching, or appliquéing.

5. Trim the pillow top to 1-1/2" larger than the pillow form.

6. Draw one diamond (square on the diagonal) around the design to "frame" the design.

7. Place a 19" x 19" layer of black fleece behind the white pillow front, with the right side of the black against the wrong side of the white, and pin the layers together.

8. Beginning on one long side of the drawn frame (not at a corner) stitch the first line, pivoting at the corners, and overlapping the beginning and ending stitching lines.

9. Stitch a second row of stitching a generous 3/8" away from the first row, again beginning and ending on one long side. Be sure to maintain the correct spacing when pivoting at the corners. (To keep all the corners nice and even, draw an extended line up through the corners. As you sew each successive row, pivot on the drawn line.)

10. Continue stitching the rows until you get approximately 1-1/2" away from the raw pillow edge.

11. On the wrong side of the pillow front, trim the excess black fleece close to the last frame stitching line.

12. To slash between stitching the lines:

a. At one of the corners, carefully make a starting cut with the small point of scissors. Be careful to cut only the top (white) layer of fleece.

b. Insert a 5/16" Mini Omnistrip cutting strip, sliding it to the next corner.

c. Carefully rotary cut on the center of the mini cutting strip, centering the slash between the stitching lines. Depending on how steady your hand is, you may choose to use a ruler for guidance.

13. Slash to the center of the next corner and remove the mini cutting strip. Again make a small clip with scissors, insert the mini cutting strip, and continue working your way around the frame until all the channels have been slashed open.

14. Finish the pillow, following the Sunflower Pillow directions, Steps #12, and 14-31 on pages 144-145.

Fleece, Pillows & Kids
A Natural Trio

Pattern courtesy of McCall Pattern Co.

Patterns courtesy of Kwik Sew Pattern Co.

Pattern courtesy of McCall Pattern Co.

Pattern courtesy of McCall Pattern Co.

Animal & Character Pillows

Kids love cozy floor pillows for everything from watching their favorite cartoon shows to overnights at grandma and grandpa's house. These pillows can also provide a soothing "touch of home" for quiet time at daycare.

Many commercial pattern companies offer floor pillows and beanbag-style pillows that work beautifully with fleece. If your child has a favorite storybook or cartoon character, use one of these patterns as a base and redraw to adapt the pattern. Just remember that these movie/book/cartoon characters are copyrighted and cannot be reproduced for resale without permission. You can make one for your special little person, but you may not resell it.

And so we come to the end of another adventure. I certainly hope you've had as much fun exploring new fleece territory as I've had leading you on new paths.

Love,
Marcy

QUICK REFERENCE GUIDE TROUBLESHOOTING, QUICK FIXES & TIPS

Since I can't provide a "Dear Nancy" advice column, I offer this section as a condensed guide for answers to common questions, problems, and situations with machines, threads, needles, fabric, and techniques. (When you read the answer, you'll probably say, "I knew that… I just forgot!")

Many problems and/or solutions cross over to each other. A stitch problem can be the result of a needle problem or thread problem. So glance through all the different areas that might pertain to your predicament or question.

This is a Quick Fix Reference Guide. I've also listed where to find more in-depth information throughout my fleece books. There you'll learn the reason for the problem and understand "the logic" so it doesn't happen again. Note: These solutions and suggestions apply to almost all of your sewing, not just fleece.

Key for finding more information:

AWP = *Adventures With Polarfleece®*
MAWP = *More Polarfleece® Adventures*
PM = *Polar Magic*

Alphabetically arranged (according to my logic!)

Adhesive Problems & Helps
AWP pages 33-34, **MAWP** pages 14-15, **PM** pages 17-19

Difficult to remove temporary iron-on stabilizers:
* Iron is too hot, causing a bond that has too strong a hold.

* Iron is held in place too long, causing a bond that has too strong a hold.
* Adhesive left in place too long. (Generally, adhesives get stronger the longer they are in place. For best results, adhere – stitch – and remove in a short time span.)

Spray adhesive not disappearing:
* Sprayed too much adhesive.

KK2000 Temporary Spray Adhesive reminder:
* Do not rinse. It is not water-soluble.

Appliqué Choices & Hints
MAWP pages 95-107, **PM** pages 126-136

Adhering appliqués to stitch in place:
* Spray KK2000 to wrong side of *appliqué* and adhere in place.

Blindhem & blanket stitch appliqué finish:
* Choose a wider (4mm or greater) stitch width to accommodate the bulk of fleece.

Blunt edge appliqué finish:
* Traditional or reverse appliqué method using the non-ravel blunt edge for a super-easy finish. Simply edgestitch appliqué in place.

Satin stitch appliqué finish:
* First stabilize fleece garment with Totally Stable before stitching appliqué (prevents wavy edges).

Border Print Design Hints

PM pages 32-40, 124-125, 141

"Think Sideways"
* Yardage = hem width needs.
* Choose fleece with excellent memory.
* Choose pattern that requires minimal or no "around-the-body stretch."

Buttonhole Problems, Hints & Helps

AWP pages 85-87, **MAWP** pages 108-116

Can't draw accurate buttonhole length on fuzzy fleece surface:
* Draw buttonhole marking on Solvy (water-soluble stabilizer) and pin or adhere in place.

Can't see drawn buttonhole line to sew buttonhole accurately:
* Draw buttonhole marking on Solvy (water-soluble stabilizer) and pin or adhere in place.

Corded buttonhole – Can't find cording to match fleece color:
* Use four to eight strands of matching thread (bunched together) as your "cording" and refer to your machine manual for corded buttonhole directions. Lengthen stitch length.

Frogmouth "gaping open" buttonholes:
* Stitch length too short. (Too dense. Lengthen stitch length to see fabric between the stitches.)

Stabilizing on a single layer of fabric:
* "Interface" buttonhole using a fleece patch of self-fabric placed against the wrong side of the garment. Place the direction of stretch in the patch opposite the direction of stretch in the garment. Sew buttonhole. Trim patch close to stitching.

Double Needle Hints

MAWP pages 36-60, **PM** pages 43-44, 46

* Arrange needle threads so they pull off the spools in opposite directions, one feeding off the front, the other off the back. This setup discourages thread tangling.

* Separate threads at every opportunity (either side of the tension disc).
* Bypass the last thread guide for one of the threads, to discourage thread tangling before entering the needles.

Drawcord Hints

AWP page 91

Can't find drawcord to match fleece?
* Use double layer of UltraSuede, cut to 3/8", edgestitched. Classy look. Great color selection.

Edge Finish Options

AWP pages 52-67, **MAWP** pages 42-44 and 122-129, **PM** pages 50-60

Cheater's Wrapped Edges:
* Use any knit fabric to wrap the raw edge of garment and stitch-in-the-ditch to secure.

Cheater's Wrapped Edges With Elastic:
* Incorporate 3/8" elastic in seam before wrapped finish. Acts like Lycra trim.

Classy Collar:
* Pintuck fleece (on the straight-of-grain), then cut out collar from the pintucked fabric.

Fat Piping:
* Cheater's Wrapped Edges using self-fabric for perfectly matching, plump edge finish.

Polar Ribbing – "Ribbing" to match:
* Pintuck the fabric to "look like ribbing."
  3.0 double needle = fine gauge ribbed look.
  4.0 double needles = moderate (regular) ribbed look.
  6.0 double needles = coarse sporty ribbed look.
* Pintuck on the straight-of-grain.

Remember: This only looks like ribbing, it doesn't act like ribbing.

Quick Fringe:
* Sandwich fleece to be fringed between two cutting mats, wrapping the fringe over one edge. Rotary cut from one mat, running onto the other.

Scalloped Edges:
❋ Blindhem stitch, mirror-imaged, with tightened needle tension. Swing of the zigzag stitch goes over the folded hem edge, creating the scallop.

Self Fabric Trim:
❋ If fabric has sufficient stretch, use self-fabric for cuffs, bottom bands, collars.

Embroidery Hints

MAWP pages 88-94, **PM** pages 71-75, 93-95

Too bulky to hoop
❋ Hoop stabilizer (rather than fleece), spray stabilizer with temporary adhesive, and adhere the fleece.

Fleece pokes up between the fill stitches:
❋ Use a topping.
❋ Use a heavier decorative thread (with appropriate needle).

Fleece color shows through thread fill stitches:
❋ Use a solid color vinyl topping.

Design has too many stitches and distorts the fleece:
❋ Add more stabilizer.
❋ Fast forward and choose only those motif features you want.
❋ Reprogram for less dense fill.

Feeding Problems

AWP pages 34-35, **MAWP** pages 13-14, **PM** pages 10-11

Fleece balking at feeding under presser foot:
❋ Lengthen stitch length.
❋ Lessen pressure on presser foot.
❋ Change to a metal presser foot (if using a plastic presser foot).
❋ Change to a walking foot.

Slipping layers of fabric:
❋ Lengthen stitch length.
❋ Lessen pressure on presser foot.
❋ Change to metal presser foot (if using a plastic presser foot).
❋ Change to a walking foot.

Needle Problems

AWP page 29, **MAWP** page 12, **PM** pages 12-14

Breaking needle:
❋ Needle too small. Go up one size larger.
❋ Bent needle. Change needle.

Noisy stitching:
❋ During embroidery: inadequate stabilization. Add more stabilizer.
❋ Adhesive build-up. Clean needle.
❋ Dull or improper needle point. Change needle.

Pattern Choices

AWP pages 37-38

❋ Choose patterns with simple lines and one-piece or two-piece garment fronts.
❋ If choosing a pattern not designed for fleece or bulky fabrics, go up one to two sizes to compensate for the bulk of the fabric and the roll of the seams.
❋ Most casual patterns suitable for coating or sweatshirting work great in fleece.

Pintuck Hints

AWP pages 106-107, **MAWP** pages 37-60, **PM** pages 41-49

❋ Stitch pintucks on the straight-of-grain (in direction of least stretch) for least distortion.
❋ Lengthen stitch length more than usual if stitching on the crossgrain (in direction of most stretch).
❋ Use presser foot with cutout underside to accommodate pintuck welts. (Pintuck foot or appliqué foot.)

Pocket Hints

AWP pages 49, 74-78

Bulky, uneven edges on patch pockets:
❋ Use the Blunt Edge Finish. Cut the pocket with a rotary cutter, removing the edge seam allowances. Fold upper facing to the inside (or outside) and topstitch in place. Tape pocket to garment using Wash-A-Way Wonder Tape. Edgestitch and topstitch in place, using the blunt cut edge as the pocket edge.

Pocket lining visible alongside welt zipper:
* Use a permanent felt tip market to color in the unsightly lining.

Perfectly welt zipper boxes:
* Count the stitches sewn at the first short end of the box and repeat the same number at the second short end.

Polar Ribbing Problems & Helps

MAWP pages 42-44, **PM** pages 41-49

Wavy "rib" lines:
* Stitch ribs on the straight-of-grain.
* Lengthen stitch length.
* Use pintuck presser foot appropriate for the double needle chosen, or use appliqué presser foot, aligning outer edge of presser foot along previously sewn rib.

"Fanning out" at cuff seam line:
* Gather sleeve hem edge to be the same size as the cuff dimension.
* Lengthen stitch length.

Rib sizes:
* 3.0 double needle = fine gauge ribbed look.
* 4.0 double needles = moderate (regular) ribbed look.
* 6.0 double needles = coarse sporty ribbed look.

Remember: This only looks like ribbing, it doesn't act like ribbing.

Golden Rules for Successful Sewing on Fleece

PM page 10

* Loosen up.
* Lighten up.
* Tape it up.
* If the conditions change, then the rules change.

Right Side/Wrong Side of Fabric

AWP page 25, **MAWP** pages 11-12, **PM** pages 12-13

* Pull on the cut edge, pulling on the crossgrain. Fabric will curl towards the wrong side.

Sculpturing Quick Hints

AWP pages 99-105, **MAWP** pages 16-32, **PM** pages 62-70

* Iron Totally Stable (iron-on tear away stabilizer) to wrong side of fleece to stabilize.
* Use decorative thread in appropriate needle.
* Use a wider (3mm to 4mm stitch width).
* Use a less dense satin stitch, i.e. increase stitch length. (You want to see a tiny bit of fleece between the stitches.)
* Use Totally Stable only on areas where the wrong side of the garment will not be visible. (Stabilizer remains in the stitches.)

Seam Problems

AWP pages 35, 44, 47-50, **MAWP** pages 12-13, **PM** page 40

Bulky seams:
* 5/8" seam allowance double topstitched flat.
* Lapped seam using Wash-a-Way Wonder Tape.
* Blunt edge finish. Perfect for pockets, collars, cuffs, lapped seams.
* Adapt pattern for "no-side-seam."

Wavy seams:
* Lengthen stitch length. If sewing "with the stretch" (or the crossgrain), lengthen as much as 4mm stitch length.

Stitch Problems

AWP page 34, **MAWP** pages 12-13

Skipped stitches:
* Needle not inserted completely.
* Needle too small. Go up one size.
* Improper needle type for the specialty thread being used. Choose an embroidery needle for rayon thread. Choose a metallic, embroidery, or topstitch needle at least size 90/14 for metallic threads.
* Check for bent or burred needle.

Test Sewing Hints

* When test sewing a seam that will likely be removed, place an off-color thread in the bobbin and use a long basting stitch length. The bobbin thread pulls out easier than the needle thread and will be more visible.

Thread Problems

MAWP page 12, **PM** page 12

Thread breaking:
* Improper needle type for the specialty thread being used. Choose an embroidery needle for rayon thread. Choose metallic, embroidery, or topstitch needle, at least size 90/14 for metallic threads.
* Check for bent or burred needle. Use a fresh needle.
* Check for rough spots on machine stitch plate. (Rub with old pantyhose. If it snags, you have a rough spot. *Gently* smooth area with crocus cloth or see your machine dealer for service.)
* Check for rough spots on the hook. (Rub hook against old pantyhose. If it snags, you have a rough spot or burr. Gently smooth area with crocus cloth or see your machine dealer for service.)
* Old thread.

Transferring Designs

MAWP pages 33-34, **PM** pages 22-31

* There is no one "right" way.
* If Totally Stable is being used to stabilize for the embellishment technique, iron Totally Stable in place as the first step.
Caution: If using KK2000 to adhere transfer medium, do not rinse. KK2000 is not water-soluble.

Zipper Problems & Hints

AWP pages 35, 69-83, and 94, **MAWP** pages 118-121

"Too long" zipper:
* Using small wire cutters, cut "to the tooth" the exact length you need. When folding excess zipper tape out of the way, fold back onto itself to create a new zipper stop.

"How to dress a naked zipper":
* Wrapped edges: (Use in an unlined garment with no facing where the zipper tape remains visible.) Encase edges of zipper tape with grosgrain ribbon, then apply zipper to garment, following pattern directions.
* Decorative-stitched zipper tape: (Use in an unlined garment with no facing where the zipper tape remains visible.) Using decorative thread and a simple satin stitch motif, embellish wrong side of zipper tape before inserting into garment.

Wavy zipper:
* Using Wash-a-Way Wonder Tape, tape rather than pin the zipper to the garment before stitching in place.
* Tape zipper to garment using an exact one-to-one ratio.
* Use a longer (3.5mm to 4mm) stitch length when stitching and topstitching zipper in place.

ABOUT THE AUTHOR

Nancy Cornwell, the "Polar Princess," has been an avid sewer and designer for over 30 years. Nancy's love of sewing and sharing her knowledge with others led her to become a nationally recognized author with her award-winning book, *Adventures With Polarfleece®*. Her second book, *More Polarfleece® Adventures*, continues to be a tremendous success, taking readers on a wonderful adventure of designing and embellishing with fleece.

Nancy firmly believes that sewing should be fun as well as a way to express yourself in what you create. To that end she has spent countless hours (as can be verified by her husband) developing techniques to make sewing easier and more fun.

Sharing her ideas, techniques, and enthusiasm is something that Nancy loves to do. She is a sought after teacher, speaker, and lecturer. Her fun and enthusiastic approach to sewing is infectious and inspires confidence in sewers of all levels. For the past 17 years she has been a featured speaker at the Sewing & Stitchery Expo in Puyallup, Wash., the largest consumer sewing event in the nation. Nancy regularly makes presentations to sold-out audiences for consumer groups, sewing exhibitions, and industry events across the country. She has also made several television appearances on programs hosted by Nancy Zieman and Sue Hausmann.

In addition to writing, teaching, and speaking, Nancy continues her own adventure by designing a collection of fleece prints for David Textiles, Inc. She is also a member of their sales and marketing department. After being a successful fabric store owner for 18 years, she enjoys helping other store owners.

As you read through this book, as well as the previous two, you will find that Nancy's love of sewing truly comes from the heart. She shares her expertise of sewing with fleece in a way that will give you confidence and encouragement to begin or continue your own adventure. As Nancy would say, go ahead, have fun… you can do it!

RESOURCES

Fleece Resources

Support your local retailers. They work hard to bring you new fabrics, notions, books, patterns, machines, ideas, and classes. If you can't find what you want, let the store owners know what you are looking for. Support your local businesses and they will always be there for you.

"Where can I find good fleece?" This is far and away the first question I hear from everyone. That's why I jumped at the opportunity to work with David Textiles, Inc. They manufacture a high quality line of fleeces (solids, prints, baby fleece, heathers, and boucles) that is readily available to *all* fabric stores across the nation. Look for the name Nordic Fleece for your assurance of quality. If your local store does not carry it, ask for it by name.

Most of the products listed in this book are readily available at your local fabric or quilting store, or at your sewing machine dealer. If you can't find the products listed, refer to these companies:

Cactus Punch, Inc.
1101 W. Grant Rd. #202
Tucson, AZ 85705
800-487-6972
http://www.cactuspunch.com
Thousands of custom and original embroidery designs, plus a series of Signature Designs from well-known sewing industry experts.

Golden Threads
2 S. 373 Seneca Drive
Wheaton, IL 60187
888-477-7718
http://www.GoldenThreads.com
Quilting paper, tremendous assortment of continuous line quilting design packs and templates.

Krause Publications
700 E. State Street
Iola, WI 54990
800-258-0929
http://www.krause.com
Major book publisher of sewing and hobby titles.

Purrfection Artistic Wearables
12323 99th Ave. N.E.
Arlington, WA 98223
800-691-4293
www.purrfection.com
Paw Prints Patterns, Pelle's See-Thru Stamps, paints, fabrics, and unique buttons.

Quilt Country
701 South Stemmons #260
Lewisville, TX 75067
972-436-7022
http://www.quiltcountry.com
Rag Time Quilt pattern as well as many other original patterns, fabrics, kits, newsletter.

Snap Source, Inc.
PO Box 99733
Troy, MI 48099
800-725-4600
http://www.snapsource.com
Long Prong snaps and The Snap Setter™ snap attaching tool.

Take Your Fleece Adventures Even Further

Adventures With Polarfleece®
A Sewing Expedition
by Nancy Cornwell

Nancy Cornwell will lead you on a sewing expedition. Explore and discover endless project possibilities for the entire family. Sew a collection of 15 projects for play, work, fashion, comfort and warmth. The heart of a fallen-away sewer will soon be recaptured and new sewers will be intrigued and inspired.

Softcover • 8-1/4 x 10-7/8 • 160 pages
200 color photos • 150 color illustrations
Item# AWPF • $19.95

More Polarfleece® Adventures
by Nancy Cornwell

Add designer touches to fleece with cutwork, sculpturing, applique, pintucking, classy edge finishes, designer buttonholes, and machine embroidery. Start off with a quick refresher course and end with a chapter filled with fun fleece projects. In between, you'll find a new world of sewing loaded with templates and patterns for the designs featured.

Softcover • 8-1/4 x 10-7/8 • 160 pages
200 color photos
Item# AWPF2 • $19.95

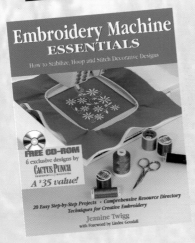

Embroidery Machine Essentials
How to Stabilize, Hoop and Stitch Decorative Designs
by Jeanine Twigg, Foreword by Lindee Goodall

Frustrated by the lack of information in your embroidery machine's instruction manual? This book will help you learn how to use your embroidery machine to its fullest potential. From choosing threads to knowing which stabilizer to pair with your fabric, you'll find helpful tips and techniques for producing creative designs. Learn to successfully hoop and stitch designs and put these skills to use creating 20 simple projects. Includes a free CD featuring 6 exclusive embroidery designs digitized by award-winning Lindee Goodall, owner of Cactus Punch®.

Softcover • 8-1/4 x 10-7/8 • 144 pages
250+ color photos and illustrations
Item# STIT • $27.95